COLLECTING

HOGAN
(FISH)

ZINT KATO
(BLUE B

THE WEST

COLLE
THE
COWBOY, INDIA N,
AND MINI NG

WILLIAM C.

CROWN PUBLISHERS,

CTING WEST

SPANISH AMERICAN, MEMORABILIA

KETCHUM, JR.

INC. NEW YORK

*To the late Robert Bishop, a good friend
and one who was always willing to explore
the outermost frontier of collecting.*

Published by Crown Publishers, Inc., 201 East 50th Street,
New York, New York 10022. Member of the
Crown Publishing Group.

CROWN is a trademark of Crown Publishers, Inc.

Book Design by June Bennett-Tantillo

Manufactured in Japan

Library of Congress Cataloging-in-Publication Data
Ketchum, William C., 1931–
Collecting the West: Cowboy, Indian, Spanish American, and mining
memorabilia / William C. Ketchum, Jr.—1st ed.
p. cm.
Includes bibliographical references and index.
1. West (U.S.)—Collectibles. I. Title.
NK805.K4728 1992
978′.0075—dc20   92-25632
                                           CIP
ISBN 0-517-57807-7

10 9 8 7 6 5 4 3 2 1

First Edition

Also by William C. Ketchum, Jr.

Early Potters and Potteries of New York State (1970, 1987)

The Pottery and Porcelain Collectors Handbook (1971)

American Basketry and Woodenware (1974)

A Treasury of American Bottles (1975)

Hooked Rugs (1976)

The Family Treasury of Antiques (1978)

The Catalogue of American Antiques (1977, 1980, 1984, 1990)

The Catalogue of American Collectibles (1979, 1984, 1990)

Collecting American Craft Antiques (1980)

Auction (1980)

Western Memorabilia (1980)

Toys and Games (Smithsonian Illustrated Library of Antiques) (1981)

Furniture, Vol. II (Smithsonian Illustrated Library of Antiques) (1981)

The Catalogue of World Antiques (1981)

Boxes (Smithsonian Illustrated Library of Antiques) (1982)

Chests, Cupboards, Desks, and Other Pieces (1982)

Pottery and Porcelain (1983)

American Folk Art of the Twentieth Century (1983)

Collecting Bottles for Fun and Profit (1985)

Collecting Toys for Fun and Profit (1985)

Collecting Sporting Memorabilia for Fun and Profit (1985)

Collecting the 40's and 50's for Fun and Profit (1985)

All American Folk Art and Crafts (1986)

American Country Pottery (1987)

Holiday Ornaments and Antiques (1990)

American Redware (1990)

How to Make a Living in Antiques (1990)

Country Wreaths and Baskets (1991)

American Stoneware (1991)

CONTENTS

INTRODUCTION

his book is intended to serve as a guide to the vast number of new collectors who have, over the past decade or so, entered the area of Western antiques and collectibles. As the popularity of Native American crafts, cowboy memorabilia, and Spanish American artifacts has increased, so have prices and the problems of fakes and reproductions. Faced with these realities, the novice may assume that there is no place in the field for him or her.

But such is not the case. A collector of modest means may accumulate a substantial hoard of interesting objects related to the Old West simply by buying carefully in areas that are not yet overpriced. As an example, most small mining mementos—lamps, picks and shovels, stock certificates

—are quite reasonably priced, as are cowboy-related items such as horseshoes and branding irons.

Moreover, for the first time, we are including in this book examples from a new and growing area often referred to as "Western kitsch." This is a vast reserve of exciting collectibles that ranges from photographs, clothing, and equipment associated with the hundreds of cowboy-and-Indian movies that have been made during this century through the promotional items such as rings, neckerchiefs, telescopes, and toy guns connected with radio figures like the Lone Ranger and Hopalong Cassidy.

An even greater range of potential collectibles reflects the nationwide interest, during the period 1910 to 1950, in almost anything associated with Western life. Clocks and bookends were made in the form of cowboys or Indians. Ashtrays and cigarette boxes were decorated with motifs such as saddles, cactus plants, lariats, and six-shooters. Portraits of Native Americans adorned pieces of art pottery, drinking glasses, even women's compacts. So numerous and varied are these items that it might be possible to furnish a small home with all the basic necessities from furniture to clothing—all of which have a Western theme!

Yet another area available to the impecunious collector is that of the later Indian collectibles that were designed by Native Americans for sale at modest prices to tourists. Such things as miniature Northwest Coast totem poles, small Pueblo bowls which were originally sold for twenty-five cents, and birchbark canoes, tipis, and tiny replicas of Navajo looms come immediately to mind.

Of course, some veteran (and wealthy) collectors will look down upon these items and those who collect them. They will call such collectibles "cheap," "trash," and "not authentic." The latter accusation is particularly inappropriate as it overlooks the fact that some of the most expensive "traditional crafts" such as Navajo blankets and the black-on-black pottery of Maria Martinez were made on order and pursuant to direction from earlier white buyers.

Once one has decided to collect Western memorabilia, the next question is where to find it. The oldest, rarest, and finest examples are, of course, available at a price from expensive shops and auction galleries. However, the adventuresome collector can often purchase appealing and valuable items elsewhere at a fraction of dealer cost. White tourists began to visit the West in substantial numbers soon after the Civil War, and the advent of the automobile after 1900 opened up the area to thousands more. Almost all brought back Indian pottery, baskets, rugs, clothing, and weapons; and these are still coming out of houses and collections throughout the United States. Collectors who will take the time to familiarize themselves with Native American crafts and will frequent house and estate sales, church bazaars, and even secondhand stores are bound, sooner or later, to come up with something very nice.

The cowboy, mining, and Spanish American items, being more restricted in both area of use and quantity, are harder to find. However, old saddles, bridles, and spurs may show up at thrift shops or even horse tack shops in the West and, though rarely, as part of Eastern collections. And remember, knowledge is not universal. A fine silver-inlaid bit or a rare New Mexican religious carving may sometimes slip through unnoticed at a rural New England or Indiana auction whereas it would be snatched up at a much higher figure in California or Wyoming. The successful collector is both knowledgeable and persistent.

He or she looks everywhere, even in the most unlikely places such as the boutique where an early Texas saddle was recently found serving as "atmosphere" for a group of Western-style skirts!

And, of course, when we talk about "kitsch," it is literally everywhere. There are probably some cowboy or Indian items in your own attic or cellar and visits to local secondhand stores, thrift shops, and yard sales will soon produce more. Since these items are so common (most were mass-produced), don't pay a great deal for them. Buy only examples in good condition and be selective while looking for good design and interesting themes. Bear in mind that if you don't set some limits, your home will soon be overflowing with memories of the Old West!

A word about fakes and reproductions:

With the exception of the ubiquitous repro brass belt buckles (Wells Fargo and the like), these are confined almost entirely to the area of Indian crafts. The makers, often Native Americans, of reproduction painted shields, headdresses, lances, bows, arrows, and war clubs (the most common items) are very skilled both at re-creating nineteenth-century form and decoration and at creating an appearance of age. If you are buying from a dealer or at auction, get a written guarantee of authenticity. If you are buying on your own, either prepare yourself by studying both authentic and fake examples in the field or be prepared to get taken once in a while. And as a general rule, always be suspicious of anything that is being offered to you at below the going market price. As in most areas, bargains in Western memorabilia can be illusory!

AMERICAN

INDIAN

COLLECTIBLES

Those who are drawn to collect objects associated with Native American culture are not venturing upon untrodden ground. As far back as the eighteenth century, Europeans and some white Americans were gathering samples of weapons, clothing, basketry, and ceramics.

One of the best known of these early collectors was Nathan Sturges Jarvis, a physician stationed at Fort Snelling, an army base near the present site of Minneapolis. Perhaps inspired by the example of General William Clark of the Lewis and Clark expedition (whose own collection has long since disappeared), Jarvis acquired a variety of objects, primarily from the Sioux, Chippewa, Winnebago, and Menominee peoples, all of whom lived in the vicinity.

As early as February 1834, Jarvis wrote to his family that "I have got some pretty Indian curiosities I will send you next spring if an opportunity affords. My room looks something like a Museum, hung around with pipes, tomahawks, war clubs & c." Anyone aware of the spirited competition among present-day collectors will hardly be surprised if not all that Jarvis found stayed in his hands. In May 1836 he complained that a box of artifacts he had shipped East had vanished, commenting that "it has doubtless been stolen by those on the boat under the supposition of its containing Indian curiosities, for which there is a great rage."

This reconstructed cliff dwelling in southwestern Colorado was originally built between 1300 and 1600. It was in homes like these that many early Anasazi makers of basketry and textiles lived. *Private collection*

In fact, none other than the famous Western painter George Catlin offered to buy the entire Jarvis collection. However, the doctor declined, and in 1848 he gave it to the New York Historical Society, thus preserving one of the earliest groupings of Native American artifacts.

Despite the subsequent dislocations of the various tribes and the bloody Indian Wars of the 1860s and 1870s, white enthusiasm for Indian crafts continued to grow. As the railroads pushed West, explorers, buffalo hunters, soldiers, and miners were joined by the first tourists. This latter group showed an especially keen appreciation for things produced by the Native Americans, a fact not lost on the operators of trading posts, the hotels built to service the railways, and even proprietors of grocery and dry-goods stores. All hastened to supply the growing need.

At first they were content to buy or take in trade such things as blankets, baskets, and pottery, which could then be sold to eastern collectors. A good example was Fred Harvey, a former freight agent for the Chicago, Burlington & Quincy railroad who opened a chain of restaurants and hotels along the Santa Fe line to which he soon added gift shops where travelers might buy Indian "curiosities."

Others, like Lorenzo Hubbell and John Moore, owners of Western trading posts, not only bought from the Indians, they directly influenced them—dictating sizes, styles, and colors to cater to the new clientele. As a result, Navajo rug makers began to create weavings incorporating motifs found in Oriental rugs, and both potters and basket makers turned out forms alien to their own cultures, often in sizes too small to serve any practical purpose but ideal for tourist sale.

Collector appreciation of Native American crafts continues undiminished and has greatly increased during the past decade with previously unheard-of prices being paid for earlier, rarer, or finer examples. Navajo rugs have brought over $100,000; single pieces of pottery $60,000 to $80,000; and rare baskets comparable sums.

This enthusiasm reflects not only respect for the high artistic quality and important historical value of much of the material, but also its great diversity. The Native Americans who occupied, and in some cases still occupy, the American West were not a single group with a single culture. While they had many similarities, they also had great differences, which were reflected in the objects they produced first for their own use and later for sale to whites.

A detail of a Native American building complex shows its construction of dried brick and rough-hewn rock. Dating about 1300 to 1600, these structures provided both shelter and protection from enemies for the early basket makers. *Private collection*

The Hopi were farmers with a complex religious system directly related to rainfall and the growing season. Their carved kachinas are cultural manifestations of that faith. Moreover, since they and other Pueblo peoples had permanent homes, they could also produce pottery for use in cooking and storage.

Plains Indians such as the Sioux and Cheyenne were of the horse and buffalo culture and constantly on the move. Pottery manufacture was not practical for them. On the other hand, the importance of the warrior and his horse led to the development of elaborate quill and beadwork garments and trappings just as centuries before, art and craft had glorified the feudal samurai of Japan and European knights of the Middle Ages.

The Navajo were herdsmen and in contact with the Spanish culture. As a result they wove their wool into remarkable blankets and floor coverings and adopted the manufacture of silver ornaments (introduced from Mexico) as a means of earning tourist dollars.

The California tribes, subsisting primarily on roots, berries, and nuts, responded to their need for light, flexible containers by producing some of the most sophisticated basketry the world has ever known; while the Northwest Coast Indians, surrounded by a wealth of woodlands, manifested their religious and social beliefs in monumental carvings.

These are but a small number of the fascinating variety of objects available to the collector. For the well-to-do there are expensive early and rare items; for the collector of modest means, an infinite number of things made for tourists during the 1920–1960 period; and those who seek contemporary crafts will find that Native American skills in many fields—particularly, silver, weaving, basketry, and ceramics—have reached new artistic heights.

NATIVE AMERICAN BASKETS

asketry is the oldest Native American craft, dating back some eleven thousand years. One of the first people known to have lived in what is now the Western United States are sometimes referred to by anthropologists as "Basket Makers," reflecting the importance of that craft in their society. Examples of conical burden baskets with sophisticated geometric patterning can be dated to the sixth century A.D.; and basketry-making techniques are basic to both Indian textile weaving and ceramics manufacture (early pots were decorated by pressing them into basketry molds).

Of course, due to their fragile nature, few early baskets have survived; and most of these are in museum collections. However, for the collector

A beaded basket from northwestern California, dated 1920–1930, is a product of the Yurok-Hupa culture. These unusual covered baskets are completely sheathed in tiny varicolored trade beads.
William Dobey

there are large numbers of fine nineteenth- and early twentieth-century examples, as well as the products of contemporary weavers who carry on the tradition at a high level. As a general rule the most valuable baskets are the rarest and the largest that have the most complex weaving or decoration. Included in this category are baskets such as the Pomo Indian feather or "treasure" baskets, which incorporate unusual materials or techniques. Moreover, since few of the earlier makers can be identified, a basket that is attributed to a respected craftsperson such as Dat So La Lee of the Washoe will bring a premium.

Native Americans have traditionally considered basketry a woman's craft, and several tribes have Creation legends describing how the gods gave this skill to women. In one of these myths, the Navajo relate how a deity approached a woman weaving a sacred wedding tray and tossed a sprig of juniper into it. The weaver responded by braiding the pattern of the folded leaf into the basket rim, thus incorporating its sacred power and creating a stylistic tradition.

This sacrosanct and ceremonial aspect of basket making is one often overlooked by white collectors. To an Indian, a basket is more than a container. Otherwise, they would have long since been replaced by commercial vessels available at trading posts. Navajo curing rituals require use of a basket; the Hopi award coiled trays or plaques to the victors in footraces; Apache bowls serve as sacred symbols during the annual girls' puberty ceremony; and the Pomo feather basket is traditionally given by a mother to her daughter, and was in past times burned on its owner's funeral pyre to ensure that it would pass with her into the afterlife.

The three general localities in which

A Pomo feather basket from central California, dates about 1900–1910. Decorated with red woodpecker feathers, abalone shell, and trade beads, these "treasure baskets" were traditionally made as gifts from mother to daughter. They are among the most desirable and most costly collector baskets. *William Dobey*

This finely woven diamond pattern bowl *(left)* and shallow basket are both attributed to the Tulare or Yokuts tribes of south-central California and dated about 1890–1910. Some of the most delicately made basketry comes from California. *Author's collection*

A basket, probably designed for cooking, has been attributed to the Salish of northern California and dated 1900–1920. Though, like other Northwest Coast tribes, the Salish made basketry for tourists, a piece like this would have been intended for tribal use. *Helen & Ezra Stoller*

most historic baskets were made and continue to be made are California, the Pacific Northwest, and the Southwestern states. Techniques, forms, and decoration often vary greatly, not only from area to area but also within each.

CALIFORNIA

Many consider baskets made by the various California tribal groups to be the most sophisticated American examples and among the finest woven anywhere. Yet there is a tremendous variation among the state's products. Northern weavers produced trays, baskets, and bowls with geometric designs such as triangles and oblongs running in bands and chevrons that were black or brown against a lighter body. The Pomo of central California also created tightly woven vessels of willow, black fern, yucca, or marsh grass; but they are best known for their feather baskets, remarkable bowls covered with feathers from the red woodpecker and decorated with tiny perforated clamshell "money" disks and dangling pendants of shaped and polished abalone shell. The finest examples date from about 1880 to 1900 and, if in good condition, will bring several thousand dollars at auction.

Another central California tribe, the Washoe, who lived near Lake Tahoe on the Nevada line, combined darker geometric patterns—particularly the triangle—with a

A large storage basket, c. 1900–1920, is probably Pomo. More than two feet high, it would have been used to store grain, vegetables, or even feathers. *Private collection*

AMERICAN INDIAN COLLECTIBLES

A 1920–1930 Navajo ceremonial or wedding tray is decorated with a design in red and black, which represents the sacred world mountains broken by the spirit path. Though these baskets are important to the Navajo, the tribe does not make them but obtains them from the Ute or other people.
Author's collection

lighter body in remarkable ovoid forms. The best-known Washoe weaver was Louise Keyser, also known as Dat So La Lee. Active from 1895 to 1925 and relying upon the support of a white patron, she produced highly individualistic baskets, which were copied by other tribal basket makers.

The Tulare of south-central California decorated their wares with bands of reddish diamonds thought to be derived from the pattern on a rattlesnake skin or with human figures holding hands ("friendship baskets"). The Mission Indians (so called because they settled about the early Spanish missions) preferred motifs featuring intertwining star forms in two colors.

We should not assume, however, that these baskets were purely decorative. Ritual use aside, the California Indians produced utilitarian baskets for storage, carrying, and even cooking. Some Pomo baskets were so tightly woven that they could be used to carry and store water. Others served as cooking pots. These were filled with water and acorn mush, then hot stones were dropped in to heat the food.

NORTHWEST COAST

The women of the Northwest Coast produced their basketry from materials quite different from those used in areas to the south. The principal fibers were cedar bark and spruce root and the products were hats and distinctive covered storage baskets as well as some odd items made for the tourist trade.

A small basketry tray with geometric decoration is probably Pima. Only six inches in diameter, this delicate piece was probably made between 1920 and 1930 for the tourist trade. *Helen & Ezra Stoller*

Vessels like this coiled basketry tray or shallow bowl (Pima, c. 1890–1910), often twelve to twenty inches in diameter, were used by Native Americans as white women would use bowls, pans, pots, or chinaware during food preparation. They were also employed by shamans or medicine men in healing the sick. *Helen & Ezra Stoller*

Long slender roots were stained with natural dyes and mixed with native grasses in finely woven twined basketry decorated with geometric patterns or pictorial images. Figurative designs had always been a characteristic of Northwest Coast work, even in the nineteenth century, when chiefs wore elaborate whaling hats intended to assure fortune on the hunt. These conical head-coverings have a distinctly Asian look and, unlike most Native American basketry, they were frequently painted—with the same abstract representations of animals and birds found on Northwest Coast carvings.

Tourist and trader interest spurred the creation of trinket baskets with lift tops and decoration that might vary from more traditional images such as the whale, salmon, or seal to an American eagle, flag, or sailing vessel. A more sophisticated version, found among the Tlingit, had a "rattle lid," the hollow center of which contained tiny pebbles or dried seeds.

Other weavers, among the Nootka, Makah, and Salish, not only turned to

Like many Apache vessels, this covered storage basket (probably Apache, c. 1900–1920) is decorated with strips of buckskin. *Helen & Ezra Stoller*

European themes, such as the reproduction in basketry of a silver tea set or a bowler hat (!), but also developed a new field: weaving upon a solid object. By 1870, travelers in Sitka, Alaska, could purchase everything from whiskey bottles to canes to seashells, all carefully covered with basketry. Such items were hardly for the purist, but their popularity is reflected in the number of pieces that exist today. They were also inexpensive. A large wine bottle with woven coverings that might have taken a day to make, retailed at fifty cents in 1870.

The Southwestern basketry bowl, probably Papago, dates 1910–1930. The Papago are among the West's most prolific basket makers, and their work is readily available to collectors. *Commission Mart*

SOUTHWESTERN BASKETRY

Many of the Southwestern tribal groups manufacture baskets, both for their own use and for sale to tourists. Most prolific are the Papago of southern Arizona, who average eight to ten thousand examples annually with a group of workers ranging in age from five to eighty years. Papago

As this 1900–1920 shallow basketry tray demonstrates, Apache baskets are often decorated with stylized human and animal figures.
Helen & Ezra Stoller

baskets, bowls, trays, and figural-shaped containers are coiled of bleached yucca or bear grass with geometric decoration of black seed pods from the "devil's claw" plant. Both their materials and their design reflect that the Papago are inheritors of the ancient Basket Maker or Anasazi traditions.

The Pima, a group closely related to the Papago, are well known for their tightly woven trays of cattail, willow, yucca, and devil's claw. These pieces feature remarkable complex geometric patterns in which alternating zigzag lines of thick and thin black against a lighter ground create the effect of spiral motion. These and other abstract patterns were probably inspired by the decoration on prehistoric Hohokam pottery found in the area.

Another group of Arizona desert dwellers, the Western Apache, have long produced shallow bowl-like baskets decorated with a central star and tall storage jars bearing a netted design interspersed with charming human and animal figures. These figures are generally applied in black on white, though a red dye made from yucca bark is sometimes used. While these vessels are primarily intended for sale, the Apache also make for tribal use piñon pitch–covered water jars as well as burden and storage baskets characteristically decorated with rawhide fringing.

Among the Pueblo dwellers the Hopi of Black Mesa are the most prolific basket makers. Pueblo work differs from that of most other Southwestern groups in that

A shallow bowl and handled basket, c. 1920–1940, are both Hopi. Typically Hopi craftspeople use more colors in their basketry than other Southwestern tribes.
Nina Ryan

This coiled storage basket, probably Paiute, 1890–1910, shows much wear and color fading. It might be considered less desirable by advanced collectors who often seek very well preserved examples. *Helen & Ezra Stoller*

some pieces are woven in wickerwork while coiled examples are characterized by thick, softly woven coils, which are often dyed in several colors.

The most characteristic Hopi vessels are bowls and sacred meal plaques, the latter resembling shallow trays. These may be decorated with geometric four-directional designs or stylized life-forms and kachina figures, and are frequently used in kachina and basket dances. Moreover, among the Second Mesa Hopi, a flat plaque is buried with each male in order to assure entrance into the afterlife.

Perhaps best known of all Southwestern forms is the large, circular Navajo ceremonial tray referred to among collectors as a "wedding basket." Full-size versions may be eighteen inches in diameter, while miniatures less than five inches across serve as fetishes. Traditional decoration consists of a jagged pattern in black surrounding a red band representing the sacred mountains of the world. Interestingly enough, these baskets, which play an important role in Navajo ritual life, are not made by the tribe. They are produced for it by the Ute and other neighboring basket makers.

Other Southwestern basket makers whose work may be of interest to collectors include the Santo Domingo and Cochiti Pueblo dwellers, who produce open wickerwork vessels, the Jicarilla Apache of New Mexico, whose coiled baskets are decorated with geometric patterns, and the Jemez, who turn out rather plain vessels of plaited yucca leaves.

POTTERY

Of the three crafts—basketry, textile weaving, and ceramics—most closely associated with Western Native Americans, the latter is most available to collectors. Pottery is more durable than either baskets or Navajo rugs and usually less expensive as well. It captured the imagination of white explorers, settlers, and traders at a relatively early period. And this enthusiasm has fueled a cottage industry that remains active today throughout much of the region.

There are two distinct categories of Indian ceramics, both originating in the Southwest. The first consists of vessels made prior to the arrival of the whites in the sixteenth century and is referred to as "precontact," "pre-

Two early Southwestern pottery bowls, both about 1880–1910, are *left,* Zuni or Acoma, and *right,* Tesuque. Often only an expert can distinguish the pots made at one pueblo from those of a neighboring one.
Private collection

European," or less exactly as "prehistoric." The second era spans the remaining period, but most collectible ceramics included therein date from the mid-nineteenth century on. Numerous different peoples living in the Four Corners area (where Utah, Colorado, Arizona, and New Mexico come together) have been involved in the development of this ceramics tradition. The modern day Pueblo tribes are the principal inheritors of the craft.

Experts estimate that about a thousand distinct ceramic styles developed in this region between the third and seventeenth centuries, most associated with the Anasazi, Hohokam, Mimbres, and Mogollon cultures. All were farming people who had abandoned hunting and gathering for the cultivation of corn, beans, and squash. For those Indians, the creation of pottery was a religious exercise as well as a craft.

The methods they employed to make and decorate their ceramics varied little from those used by many twentieth-century Pueblo potters. Vessels were constructed by hand using the coil method (Native Americans did not develop the potter's wheel) and were decorated either by painting designs on the surface or by corrugating it with the fingers or with tools. In either case, the decoration was based on earlier basketry and weaving designs.

Pieces to be painted were scraped smooth, coated with a clay slip, and embellished with abstract designs applied with a brush made of chewed yucca leaf. Paints were mineral or carbon based. Known forms included bowls; cooking, storage, and seed jars; dippers and scoops; pitchers, canteens, and drinking vessels. All pieces were baked in surface fires rather than in kilns.

While the numerous design variations are beyond the scope of this book, certain generalities may be made about this ware. Most Mogollon pottery was of polished

brown or red firing clays, sometimes embellished with broad bands of contrasting red or brown. Hohokam vessels often had a buff body upon which curling, featherlike designs in red appeared. Anasazi craftsmen developed a white or grayish white body upon which they worked highly abstract geometric motifs in black slip derived from their basketry and textile weavings. However, by 1300 they also began using polychrome decoration in purple, black, and green on red, orange, or yellow slip, the forerunner of modern Pueblo motifs.

The Mimbres also used a black slip on a whitish base to produce precise geometric patterns, but they went beyond this design to turn out vessels with remarkable pictorial representations of men and animals. Among these are charmingly stylized insects, birds, frogs, coyotes, and what appear to be crayfish. All have a wonderful animated quality that has great appeal for collectors and has made this uncommon ware

Prizes of a collection are two Southwestern pueblo bowls: *left,* with incised decoration, San Juan, c. 1930–1945; *right,* with original Santa Clara label and dating, c. 1920–1940. *Author's collection*

A group of Hopi pottery objects, all c. 1910–1930, are *left to right:* a bowl with an abstract bear claw design; an olla with abstract bird design; another bowl with bear claw design; a vase with bird wing decoration, signed Jeanette (Nampeyo); and a bowl signed Nellie Nampeyo. Both these women are descendants of the famous Hopi potter Leah Nampeyo. *Private collection*

among the most expensive of all Native American ceramics.

Precontact pottery like this is available at auction and through dealers, but its collection is controversial in some quarters. Much of it has been acquired through excavation and destruction of ancient sites by "pot hunters" who are often little better than grave robbers. For example, many Mimbres vessels bear a "kill hole" in the center reflecting the fact that the pots were buried with their deceased owners. The pot was placed over the face and then ceremoniously "killed" by poking a round hole in the base. A bowl so disfigured could originally have been acquired in only one way, by violating a grave.

Native American spokesmen understandably object to the collection of such pieces. They are joined by archaeologists, who point out that trade in precontact ceramics encourages grave robbing, which in turn destroys any chance of obtaining meaningful historical information from sites so treated.

There is no indication that these objections will seriously affect most dealers and collectors; and, of course, most items offered for sale were collected years ago under circumstances unknown today. Nevertheless, collectors should be aware of the problem as well as the possibility of claims growing out of the acquisition of newly excavated vessels.

Interest in modern Indian pottery arose in the 1870s as railroads pushed their way into the Southwest, bringing tourists eager for souvenirs. One of the first to capitalize on this demand was the Fred Harvey Company, which had established hotels and restaurants at station stops along the Santa Fe–Atchison-Topeka line through what is now Arizona and New Mexico.

Harvey's firm encouraged many native

The ceramic "storyteller" figure has been attributed to the Cochiti pueblo potter Helen Cordero, c. 1930–1950. These charming pieces are popular with collectors of all ages.
Helen & Ezra Stoller

A Zuni pottery basket dates between 1930 and 1940. This was one of the many nonnative forms developed with the encouragement of white traders and tourists. *Author's collection*

Pieces like this large twelve-inch black pottery storage jar from the Santa Clara pueblo, c. 1910–1930, were usually intended for use within the community rather than for sale. *Author's collection*

potters to sell their wares at curio shops located in his establishments and to make pieces that would appeal to this trade. Thus, the traditional large storage and cooking pots were joined by smaller (and less expensive) vessels and by such non-Indian items as ashtrays, tumblers, tiles, plates, and cups and saucers. Many such items were sold for twenty-five or fifty cents apiece.

At the present time, collectors have available to them pottery made at about eighteen different pueblos. The output of some pueblos is minimal and the work of others is largely out of favor; but for most, a thriving trade finds eager buyers. Among the most desirable examples are those bearing the signature of a highly regarded craftsperson, living or dead. Among the most famous of these are Leah Nampeyo of the Hopi village of Hano on Arizona's First Mesa, and Maria and Julian Martinez from San Ildefonso Pueblo near Santa Fe, New Mexico. All three were innovators who not only placed their stamp of genius on all pottery subsequently made by their people but also made a national and even international impact.

HOPI: In 1895, archaeological excavations at the site of Sikyatki, a fifteenth-century Hopi village, revealed the presence of spectacular pottery decorated with geometric elements, including abstract feather and bird forms. Leah Nampeyo, a potter whose husband was working on the project, seized upon these pieces as inspiration for a line of new Hopi pottery featuring her interpretation of the ancient motifs.

Nampeyo received wide recognition during her lifetime and, as is the Pueblo custom, she trained other family members in the craft, fully recognizing that it would serve them well financially. As one of

Acoma pottery such as this storage jar, c. 1910–1920, is coveted not only for its abstract decoration but also for its ceramic body, which is the most thinly potted of all pueblo ceramics. *Author's collection*

her great-granddaughters later remarked, ". . . the Old Lady [Nampeyo] told us that we should learn to make the pottery because it would be something to provide us a living."* Nampeyo's descendants and other Hopi craftspersons have continued to turn out ware in variations of her typical style, sometimes incorporating kachina figures, the other folk element closely associated with their people.

SAN ILDEFONSO: Even better known is the work of Maria and Julian Martinez of San Ildefonso Pueblo. Though they also made polychrome ceramics with geometric and pictorial designs, this husband-and-

---

* Quoted in John E. Collins, *Nampeyo, Hopi Potter: Her Artistry and Her Legacy* (Flagstaff, Ariz.: Northland Press, 1974).

While the design of this rug, c. 1930–1950, is highly unusual, like most Navajo textiles this piece cannot be assigned to a particular weaver or locality. *Helen & Ezra Stoller*

thereafter the Navajo wove only wearing and saddle blankets.

The years 1800 to 1880 are referred to by dealers and collectors as the classic period, and blankets from this era may bring more than $100,000 at auction. The earliest examples, from 1800 to about 1850, were finely woven in simple striped patterns running across the narrow portion of the piece. Colors initially were limited. The natural white, brown, and black of wool might be altered by the addition of a dull red made from alder bark and mountain mahogany, a lemon yellow from alum, and blue from indigo obtained in trade with the Mexicans. Also, by the 1820s, a commercially manufactured English flannel, known among Spanish traders as bayeta, had appeared in

This Navajo saddle blanket dates c. 1910–1930. Saddle blankets are still made and used by the Navajo, though most earlier examples have been destroyed or damaged through wear.
Helen & Ezra Stoller

the Southwest. Navajo weavers unraveled the bayeta, dyed it, and spun it into their blankets along with native wool.

By the 1850s, and at least in part due to Spanish American influence, the Navajo added alternating stripes in varying colors, diamonds, and zigzag patterns to the plain stripes of the first phase. These blankets attracted the attention not only of whites but also of the Plains Indian tribes, who became major consumers of Navajo textiles, especially the so-called chief's blankets.

These latter differed from their predecessors not only in design but also in form. They were wider than they were long, as were Hopi and other Pueblo textiles. There are three phases reflected in the development of the chief's blanket. The first blan-

Among the most popular of Native American craft objects are the brightly colored late-nineteenth-century "eyedazzler" Navajo blankets. A detail of one is shown here. *Private collection*

A Navajo saddle blanket in a hexagonal twill weave, c. 1910–1930, is one of the more complex twill weaves that are not always recognized as Navajo in origin, which are usually a simpler weave.
Helen & Ezra Stoller

kets were characterized by broad horizontal stripes in black and white, which alternated with patterned bands. Second-phase examples are recognized by an elaboration of the patterned banding, usually through the addition of darker bars or ribbon-form designs. In the third phase, the bands are overlaid with serrated or terraced diamonds or triangles in groups of three.

Though not, of course, made for the exclusive use of chiefs, these wearing blankets were expensive and were considered an important trade item. Indians wearing them appear in numerous nineteenth-century photographs. They are highly prized by contemporary collectors.

Yet another innovation was the "eyedazzler," a blanket form that was developed in direct response to changing circumstances in the Southwest. As railroads reached the area in the early 1880s, they brought with them a variety of trade goods, including the Pendleton blanket and other manufactured textiles. Indian customers favored these over native wares, forcing weavers to seek a new market.

Encouraged by traders and an increasing number of tourists, the Navajo modified their designs to suit white tastes. Newly available aniline dyes, either packaged or in the form of factory-spun yarn called "Germantown" (since much came from that area of Pennsylvania), allowed them to use a variety of bright, often garish hues. The "wedge weave," whose exaggerated serrations and zigzag pattern was learned from New Mexican craftsmen, was transformed into the eyedazzler, a boldly colored, predominantly diamond-form blanket. The blanket consisted of contrasting color blocks and multidirectional design elements that were combined to create optical compositions that magically changed their form depending upon the viewer's position.

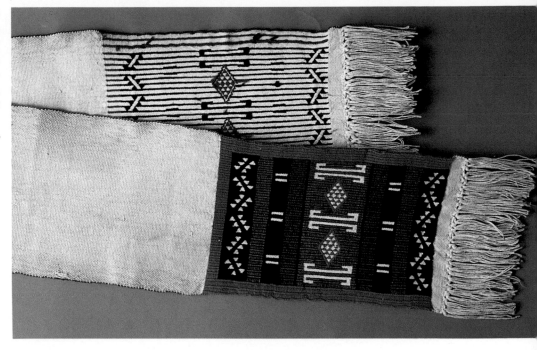

This Hopi woven cotton man's dance sash has been dated to 1900–1910. Pueblo weaving antedates that of the Navajo and is also more complex. The sash design traditionally takes the form of a stylized head of the Broadfaced kachina.
Helen & Ezra Stoller

Moreover—and again to suit the new and growing market—the blankets became rugs, table and pillow covers, and stair runners. Borders, never before found on traditional blankets, appeared, and pictorial elements were woven into the fabric. Best known are the Yei rugs, which picture Navajo ritual figures ("Yeis") and sandpainting rugs with compositions based on the ephemeral sacred designs drawn in sand as part of religious exercises. Both forms have been criticized by many Navajos as sacrilegious, but they are still made.

The new white market brought prosperity to some weavers, but it also brought a decline in quality—particularly since some trading post proprietors insisted on buying rugs by the pound rather than the piece. Weaving deteriorated, and strong colors and non-Indian motifs, such as Oriental and even Art Deco rug patterns, took the place of traditional motifs.

There were other turn-of-the-century traders, though, such as Lorenzo Hubbell of Ganado, Arizona, John B. Moore of Crystal, New Mexico, and George Bloomfield of Toadlena, New Mexico, who encouraged use of natural dyes and tribal designs. Modern rugs such as those referred to as Two Gray Hills, Ganado, Four Corners, and Tec Nos Pas reflect this blend of traditional elements and Western design.

HIDE AND LEDGER DRAWINGS

ative Americans were visually oriented and, lacking a written language, they turned early to pictorial imagery as a way of conveying information. The petroglyphs, or rock carvings, found throughout much of North American often date back over a thousand years, while sixteenth-century murals or wall paintings have been found at the ancient Hopi villages of Awatovi and Kawaika-a.

Central to this form of communication was the pictograph, a figure or group of figures that commemorated an important event, marked a territorial boundary, or served as a memory aid to storytellers and oral historians. Among the Plains Indians it was customary to use pictographs

to decorate various objects made of buffalo, deer, elk, or antelope hide.

As early as 1541, a member of a Spanish expedition that traveled into what is now the state of Arkansas reported that "[t]he house [tipi] of the Cacique [Chief] was canopied with colored deer-skins, having designs drawn upon them, and the ground was likewise covered in the same manner as if with carpets."

Not only tipis but tipi liners, dance and war shields, and buffalo robes were similarly embellished. The earliest existent hide drawing is on a Mandan buffalo robe collected by the Lewis and Clark expedition in 1805. It is covered with stick-figure representations of men and horses, and records a battle fought between the Mandan and the Sioux about 1797.

The most ancient skin drawings are highly schematic, with stick-leg horses shown in profile and men with rectangular ("playing card") bodies, viewed frontally. However, contact between the Mandan and Sioux (the chief Plains artists) and whites soon led the former to draw more realistic

SCULPTURAL FORMS

ative Americans have a highly developed artistic sense. Among most tribes, aesthetics dictated that even humble everyday objects be shaped with an eye for beauty as well as utility. This philosophy is best seen in the work of the Northwest Coast tribes, where almost everything made for communal purposes became a sculptural statement.

All Native American art is, in the final analysis, religious art; this is particularly the case with the work of the Haida, Tlingit, Nootka, and other tribes of the coastal area stretching from Washington State to Alaska. However, because of the complex class structure that existed among these groups, art also became a form of social control reflecting the power and prestige of the "royal families" and distinguishing them from others.

Nobility was conferred by inheritance: by the claim to certain connections with spirits, usually of an animal nature, or from noble ancestors. Noble families had power and privilege but they also had obligations, such as the preservation of tribal legends, songs, and dances and the obligation to hold ceremonial gift-giftings, or "potlatches."

An important part of this system was the carving, usually from native cedar, of symbolic items such as effigy columns, house posts, and, most familiar to collectors, totem poles. These were shaped and painted in a highly abstract way, referred to by art historians as the "form line" manner. The artists incorporated into their work the almost unrecognizable figures of animals such as Bear, Otter, Frog, Eagle, Killer Whale, Raven, and Mountain Lion, who were believed to have supernatural powers that might be transferred to humans. Indeed, under certain circumstances people, particularly shamans or priests, might assume both the attributes and form of these guardian deities.

This concept of transformation and the close alliance with animal guardians permeated Northwest Coast art. There were extraordinary articulated masks worn by dancers who were thought to assume the character of Bear, Eagle, or the mythical two-headed water monster, Sisiutl. There were war helmets, clan hats (embellished

A ceremonial club of cedar, Northwest Coast , mid-twentieth century, has a knob in the form of a carved and painted man's head. Its shaft bears a representation of a frog.
Frank Carbone

SCULPTURAL FORMS

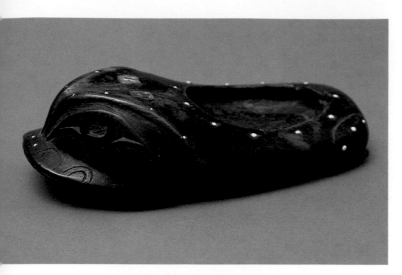

This small animal-form food or eating bowl is made of painted cedar with inlay of abalone shell and white trade beads as well as incised decoration. It originates from the Northwest Coast, c. 1900–1910. *Frank Carbone*

with rings of woven cedar bark marking the number of potlatches their owners had sponsored), headdress frontlets to be worn on ceremonial occasions, sacred pipes of wood or carved stone, elaborate feast spoons, and the shaman's rattles and charms, which served either to summon personal demons or to protect against their excesses.

All were carved, often with the addition of abalone inlay or paint applied with extraordinary sensitivity, in a manner so sophisticated as to rank this work among the finest mankind has ever produced. The creators of these objects held an exalted status, and were commissioned to work not only within their own tribes but among their neighbors as well.

A Haida oil or food bowl of carved cedar, c. 1920–1940, is a twentieth-century version of a storage form popular at least as early as 1850. *Carl Hotkowiski*

AMERICAN INDIAN COLLECTIBLES

One side of a two-faced
shaman's rattle of carved and
painted cedar (possibly Tlingit,
early to mid-twentieth century)
appears to depict the sacred
Sparrow Hawk. Seeds sealed
within the body provide the
rattle sound. *Frank Carbone*

The rattle's other face is that of
a human, reflecting the duality
of nature depicted in much
Northwest Coast art.
Frank Carbone

A Northwest Coast, possibly Haida, shaman's rattle of carved and painted cedar from the third quarter of the twentieth century is in the form of Raven, regarded as a wise counselor to the shaman. *Frank Carbone*

The reverse of the Raven rattle shows human and animal faces, which assume a different aspect depending on the angle at which the rattle is held. *Frank Carbone*

The form-line style dominated the Northwest Coast culture and was applied not only to overtly ceremonial items but also to a range of objects such as storage chests, boxes of various sizes, shell-inlaid serving bowls, weapons such as iron or copper daggers, war clubs made from elk antler, and even canoe and house construction.

Since wood was readily available, it was the material of choice. However, heads and totems carved from limestone and other rock have been excavated, and these indicate that the basic Northwest Coast style may have developed at least a thousand years ago. Modified over time, it remains strong today. Captain James Cook acquired masks at Nootka Sound in 1778 that are in the same style as those sold to twentieth-century visitors. Changes, of course, were inevitable. During the so-called golden age (roughly 1840 to 1870), craftsmen took advantage of new Western tools to carve monumental totems; the Haida specialized in figures of soft argillite and ivory that had great appeal to white buyers. Prosperity brought about through the fur trade resulted in commissions for a growing artist class. And though this time passed, the Northwest maintains a vital artistic tradition, the products of which have great appeal for many collectors.

Outside of the Northwest area, the best-known Native American sculpture is the kachina of the Southwestern Pueblos, which are discussed in the next section. However, most Western Indians did some carving. California Indians centered in the Los Angeles–Santa Barbara region shaped soapstone replicas of fish such as sailfish and swordfish as well as human figurines. What these objects were used for is unknown today.

Among the Plains Indians, even the most utilitarian objects could be things of beauty: a pair of snowshoes, delicately shaped and embellished with tufts of trade cloth; a lethal but skillfully carved war club studded with brass tacks and shaped like a gun stock; a horse-form dance fetish; or a flute (traditionally used in courting) with incised and painted decoration.

Also of great interest are mirrors of which two kinds are known—both dating as far back as the 1830s. Dance mirrors—used in ceremonial dances—were elongated, somewhat resembling a letter opener. The wooden framework was covered with incised decoration and often painted, while the narrow oval mirror itself was designed to reflect light rather than a human visage.

Oblong mirrors with chip-carved decorations and rounded "lollipop" handles were based on European prototypes and were used in applying facial paint. An early commentator, the Reverend Pond, noted that "they spent much time in painting their

A pair of painted cedar model totem poles, twelve inches high, were made in the Northwest Coast in about 1920–1930. Full-sized versions embodied the ancestral crests of tribal families. Models like these have long been a popular tourist item. *Frank Carbone*

This is a detail of a "talking stick" or speaker's staff of carved and painted cedar made by the Nootka craftsman Joe David about 1980. Essentially a sign of high office, the staff is carried by chiefs and others of rank in the community at ceremonial functions.
Frank Carbone

This carved and painted Northwest Coast cedar dance mask in the form of a mosquito was made by Francio Home in 1979. Many gifted contemporary carvers carry on the area's sculptural tradition.
Frank Carbone

An Omaha Sioux dance board of carved wood, decorated with horsehair, leather, and brass tacks, dates c. 1880–1900. Native Americans held these boards, which possessed religious significance, in their hands while performing tribal dances. *Private collection*

Peter Moon of Kingcome Inlet carved and painted this Northwest Coast cedar dance mask in eagle form about 1970–1980. Masks like this are used in performing dances, which pass cultural traditions down from one generation to the next. *Frank Carbone*

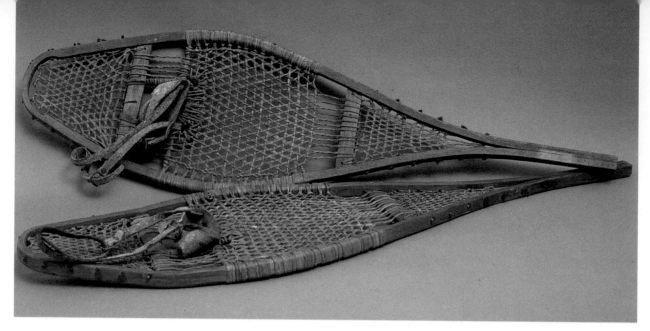

Argillite, a form of slate, was used to carve the Northwest Coast totem pole, possibly Haida, c. 1910–1930, shown here in detail. *Frank Carbone*

A pair of hand-formed snowshoes is Chippewa, c. 1900–1920. These essential items were made by bending hardwood into the proper shape and then weaving a netting of thin buckskin strips between the frames. Decoration was provided by tufts of red trade cloth. *Private collection*

faces with various kinds of paints and carried little mirrors hanging in their girdles, of which they made great use. . . ."

Perhaps most significant of all Plains Indians carving were the pipe and pipe stem. Native Americans regarded the pipe as a sacred object and the smoking of it a religious ritual. They cultivated nearly a dozen species of tobacco; these might also be mixed with other substances such as sumac leaves, bark, or manzanita.

Prehistoric carved soapstone, sandstone, or bauxite pipes found in Oklahoma were of large size, sometimes weighing as much as eighteen pounds, and probably intended only for public use. On the other hand, every individual Plains tribesman had his own pipe. There were also particularly sacred pipes owned by the entire community in common.

Plains pipe heads were and still are

This northern Plains Indian pipe is carved from catlinite and inlaid with pewter, with a wooden stem. Elbow-form pipes were made and used by most Plains tribes, and among some they became a major art form. *Private collection*

A rare sculptural piece is this combination war club and quirt or riding whip, Sioux, c. 1870–1880. It is hand-carved, touched with red paint, and decorated with feathers and bits of leather. *Private collection*

carved from catlinite, a soft red stone first described in the 1830s by the artist George Catlin. This material has been quarried since the 1600s at what is now Pipestone National Monument in southwestern Minnesota. Early examples were tubular, the next elbow-shaped, and by the 1800s a T-shaped form had evolved.

Decoration of the pipe head may consist of inlay in tin or lead set into channels in the stone body, or of sculptural carving through which the pipe assumes the form of a man or animal or is embellished with small figurines. Pipe stems are equally well designed. Carved from wood, they are covered with incised and painted decoration, cut in a corkscrew shape, or even carved in complex patterns as in the case of the "puzzle stem" which is so convoluted that only its maker knows how the smoke gets from the bowl to the mouthpiece.

KACHINAS

Among the most popular of Southwestern artifacts are the colorful and varied figures referred to by many collectors as "kachina dolls." Though certainly doll-like in appearance, the kachinas are not playthings, but serve a more complex purpose.

The term *kachina* refers initially to several hundred different supernatural beings and ancestors venerated by the Hopi and Zuni tribes of Arizona and New Mexico. The kachina cult developed among the Hopi of the Three Mesas area as early as the fourteenth century. It became progressively more complex until by the time white settlers arrived, it had evolved into a series of rituals involving members of every clan and family.

A carved and painted cottonwood Hopi Snake Dancer kachina dates from 1900 to 1910. There are more than three hundred standard kachina figures as well as another two hundred or so that the Hopi may occasionally carve. *University of Colorado Museum*

A slightly later (1920–1940) Hopi kachina, Palhik Mana, or Corn Grinding Maiden, is also of carved and painted cottonwood. Like other kachinas, she has a specific role in dances and ceremonies, in this case those relating to crops and harvest. *Brooklyn Children's Museum*

It extends from the Soyal ceremony, which celebrates the winter solstice, through late July, when, the year's harvest assured, the Niman or "going home" celebration marks the departure of the spirits for their homes in the San Francisco Mountains north of present-day Flagstaff, Arizona.

The Hopi and Zuni believe that the kachina spirits visit them each year, and upon their yearly return from the underworld the various kachinas are represented by members of the Kachina Society, men who wear elaborate masks and costumes mimicking the form and features of the deities. The masks, stored in underground rooms called kivas, which are also used for secret portions of the ritual, are considered sacred

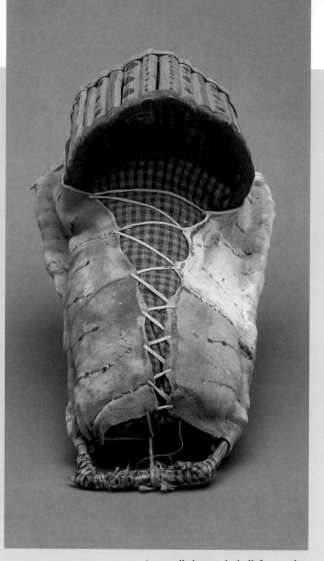

This unidentified Native American doll, c. 1920–1930, has a cloth body, horsehair, eyes, nose, and mouth of beads, beadwork-decorated flannel dress and oilskin headband holding feathers.
Brooklyn Children's Museum

A cradleboard doll from the Great Basin area of the Northwest has been dated to 1830–1880. Its limbless cloth body is wrapped in a wool hooded blanket; the hardwood cradle frame, bent into shape, is partly covered with homespun cotton cloth and buckskin. Exposed wood shows traces of old paint. This is an extremely rare and early example, intended for tribal use.
Brooklyn Children's Museum

This early Navajo doll, dated between 1880 and 1890, has a stuffed muslin body and limbs, a painted leather face, braided silk hair, trade bead earrings, and a print cotton blouse and apron over a long skirt. It was probably intended for a member of the tribe.
Brooklyn Children's Museum

ver and turquoise jewelry and concho belts with which they are adorned. Unlike most other Indian dolls, the female figures have elaborate hairdos.

Greatly different are the carved wooden dolls of the Northwest Coast. These are no warm and loving playthings, but stark sculptural figures with gaping mouths and lower lips swollen by the labrets regarded as a mark of beauty among local tribes. Carved by the same craftsmen who produced the dance masks and totem poles of the Haida and Tlingit, these dolls are true works of art, their abstract features embellished with painted eyes and eyebrows. Hair is usually human or animal, and while the hands and feet may be fully developed, the body, which is clothed in a simple trade cotton gown, is not. Decorative accessories are usually minimal, perhaps a necklace or bracelet of shells.

The earliest known Northwest Coast dolls date to the 1840s, and these must be considered rare. Post-1900 dolls are much more common and are more broadly modeled, perhaps reflecting their makers' compromise with the tourists' preference for more "charming" dolls.

A painted wooden trade sign for a dry goods store (c. 1900–1910) features a mounted Plains Indian warrior. The legendary strength and courage of the Indian brave was used to promote many commodities having nothing at all to do with Native American culture.
Sharon W. Joel

A carved and painted wood whirligig has been dated between 1920 and 1950. During the early 1900s one of the most popular forms of whirligig or wind toy was the Indian paddling a canoe. Examples are still being made today.
Private collection

AMERICAN INDIAN COLLECTIBLES

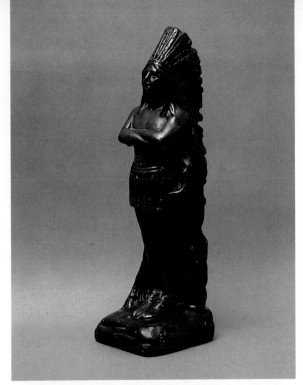

A fast-growing new collecting area is twentieth-century chalkware, like this painted cast chalk or plaster novelty figure in the form of an Indian brave, c. 1920–1940. Statuettes of this nature were awarded as prizes at carnival and circus games of chance. *Private collection*

in which Indian "cures" were sold as well as the advertising posters, flyers, and almanacs published to promote them.

Nor was quack medicine all that the Indian image promoted. The evil of tobacco became associated with Native Americans through the cigar store Indian or tobacconist's figure that once stood outside (and sometimes, in a smaller version, inside as well) every tobacco and pipe shop in the country. Often skillfully carved and brightly painted, these figures, of chiefs or maidens, offered a package of "seegars" or a few sheaves of tobacco to every passerby. The message was not always well received in the West, where Indian wars and their memory lingered longest. Several communities had to remove their promotional devices because cowboys had a nasty habit of shooting them up while on a Saturday-night binge! Nevertheless, enough cigar-store Indians have remained to provide the well-to-do collector with another form of Indian memorabilia.

A carved and painted wooden cigar-store Indian was a frequent sight in about 1880 to 1900. Association of the Native American with the cultivation and smoking of tobacco resulted in these figures being the preferred trade signs for tobacconist's shops. *Museum of American Folk Art*

A painted sheet-iron sign for a private camp dates from 1900–1930. As whites took to the woods in the late nineteenth century, they appropriated the original forest dwellers as decorative motifs for their summer homes. *Private collection*

This pair of "Skookum" dolls was made by the H. H. Tammen Co. of Los Angeles 1920–1930. The dolls have painted composition heads, stuffed cloth bodies, human hair wigs, and wooden feet and are clad in flannel blankets. The man wears felt pants and the woman a cotton print dress; both have leather shoes. The Skookums are the most popular of white-made "Indian" dolls. *Brooklyn Children's Museum*

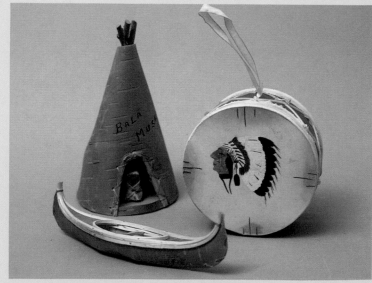

This grouping of typical tourist items made by Indians for sale to white tourists includes, from *left to right,* a birchbark canoe, birchbark tipi with carved wooden figure, and painted rawhide and wood drum. All the pieces, c. 1930–1950, are actually Indian-made and quite desirable, unlike current examples, which may have been produced in Korea or Hong Kong. *Stephanie A. Ross*

An Indian doll made about 1910–1920 by the Heubach Company in Germany has a porcelain head and arms, kid body, mohair wig, and buckskin cape, dress, and moccasins. By the early 1900s even European toy manufacturers were producing images of Native Americans. This is one of the most sensitive and authentic. *Brooklyn Children's Museum*

Even whites tried their hands at making totem poles. This carved and painted wooden example was produced by a Seattle, Washington, Boy Scout in 1938. *Private collection*

This 1950–1960 painted sheet tin-and-composition windup toy is from West Germany. The game of cowboys and Indians has spawned a vast number of collectible Western images, some of which bring high prices today. *Private collection*

A Northwest Bay wool blanket, made around 1900–1920, has characteristic beaver marks. Originally used in trade with Western tribes, these blankets bore slashes indicating the number of beaver for which each would be exchanged. Equally collectible are the more colorful Pendleton blankets. *Private collection*

Two mugs carved from hardwood are decorated with lithographed images of Indians, c. 1910–1930. Pieces like this were sold as souvenirs at well-known vacation spots such as Yellowstone Park, the Catskill Mountains, and Mount Whitney. *Stephanie A. Ross*

Folk art collectors are also particularly aware of the number of weathervanes and whirligigs with an Indian theme. In fact, one of the oldest existent American vanes, made by Shem Drowne of Boston in 1716, is in the shape of an Indian archer. A far more common form throughout the United States is the whirligig, which features an Indian in a canoe, his arms terminating in paddles that whirl in the wind, creating the illusion of furious rowing. Though often thought of as old, most of these were created during the 1930s and 1940s, when plans for building them appeared regularly in such magazines as *Popular Mechanics*.

Other products of white society became a part of Indian life, often replacing their native counterparts. A good example would be Pendleton and Hudson's Bay blankets, which gradually replaced Navajo blankets as the garment of choice among the Plains tribes. Today, these coverings have also become extremely popular among collectors.

A second broad category of "not quite" Indian collectibles are those objects made by Native Americans for sale to whites but which have no substantial connection to any continuing Indian craft tradition. For decades Western Indians have made and sold, either directly or through trading posts, such things as miniature tipis, canoes, bows and arrows, and drums. These are usually

This oil-on-board folk art painting of an Indian camp was made sometime between 1890 and 1920. Once Native Americans were no longer perceived as a threat, whites became nostalgic about their way of life. Paintings like this one depicted the ideal-ized Indian life-style.
Private collection

A page from an early 1900s catalog of the Pendleton, Oregon, Woolen Mills gives some idea of the variety of blankets produced by the firm. These woolen fleece blankets proved extremely popular among Native American buyers.
Pendleton Woolen Mills, Inc.

made of natural materials. Drums, for example, are of hide stretched over a shaped wooden frame. Decoration is usually oriented toward the consumer with such things as the head of an Indian in a war bonnet or a group of dancers and, sometimes, even the name of the locality from which the souvenir came.

Some white collectors who seek more authentic craft objects are offended by these things and view them as caricatures; but they overlook the fact that once Indians began to manufacture for a white market in the nineteenth century, it was inevitable that they sought to produce for the entire white market, not just an elite fringe. Moreover, these drums, tents, dolls, and other items have two distinct virtues. They are often charming in themselves and, as yet undiscovered by most collectors, they remain inexpensive in a field where prices for most desirable examples are rapidly eliminating the collector of modest means.

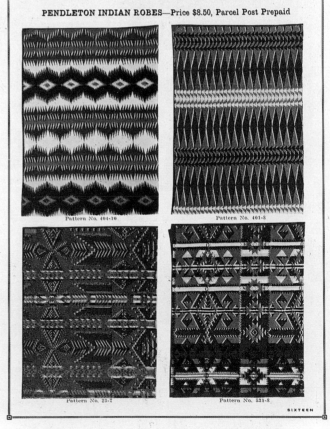

PENDLETON WOOLEN MILLS, PENDLETON, OREGON

PENDLETON INDIAN ROBES—Price $8.50, Parcel Post Prepaid

Pattern No. 404-10. Pattern No. 401-8

Pattern No. 23-7 Pattern No. 531-8

SIXTEEN

COWBOY

COLLECTIBLES

Unlike the case with Native American crafts, collector enthusiasm for cowboy-related objects is a recent phenomenon. It is only within the past decade that a substantial number of collectors have begun to seek out materials relating to the Old West. As a result, we are not yet seeing the astronomical price rises so typical in the American Indian field. True, a saddle by a well-known maker such as Wyoming's J.S. Collins can bring $5,000, a rare horsehair bridle might reach the $7,000 mark, and individually handmade spurs are regularly valued at between $300 and $3,000. Yet these hardly compare with the frequent $10,000-plus figures realized by sellers of American Indian baskets, pottery, and textiles.

Cowboy collectibles fall generally into two broad categories: objects used by men who actually rode the range, and objects that served as costumes or props in the popular cowboy movies of the 1920–1960 era. The latter recall the days of Tom Mix, Roy Rogers, and Gene Autry as well as such later figures as John Wayne and Clint Eastwood.

Authentic period cowboy memorabilia can be further divided into horse tack (such as saddles, bridles, and bits) and cowboy clothing and equipment. Most important in the latter category are hats, boots, and chaps. Rifles and pistols, which can bring astronomical figures at auction, are only of peripheral interest here. They are largely the province of gun collectors rather than those who seek cowboy materials, and the most sought-after items are associated with lawmen, gunmen, and soldiers rather than ranch hands.

Some collectors also express interest in those objects which reflect collateral aspects of the cowboy's life—the cooking utensils he used, the musical instruments that served to brighten the lonely hours on the prairie, and the drinking and gambling devices that often separated him from his meager earnings.

One of the most attractive things about working cowboy gear is its age; another is its provenance. Many items such as saddles, bridles, and even hats can be traced back well before 1900, making them antiques in the real sense. Moreover, manufacturers, most of whom were located west of the Mississippi, frequently marked their wares. Brand names were stamped into iron or brass bits and spurs or were burned or embossed on saddles and chaps. Research in this field, while relatively recent, has already allowed dealers and collectors to identify and date large numbers of objects. For those who seek artifacts by known makers (something extremely rare in pre-1920

Indian items), this is a definite advantage.

Movie props and costumes (often referred to in the trade as "cowboy funk") as well as toys, musical instruments, and a vast array of household goods that relied on Old West nostalgia for their sales appeal, offer a second and infinitely expanding category.

Of most importance are those items associated with Western movies, for it was this film genre that kept the Western mystique alive during the early twentieth century—a time when the cowboy and his horse were vanishing from the plains. As Jay Hyams says in his epical *The Life and Times of the Western Movie*, "the first true movie was a western, and the history of western movies is in large part the history of moviemaking in the United States."

Though certain Western movie memorabilia can be costly (the saddle for Roy Rogers's horse Trigger would probably bring more than any nineteenth-century example), many of these objects remain inexpensive—in part because collectors are just discovering them. Such "cowboy kitsch" represents the new frontier in Western collecting, and it offers the collector of modest means an opportunity to get into the action, often via his local flea market, junk store, or yard sale rather than through the usual and more costly route of auction or dealer.

COWBOY HORSE TACK

or the cowboy, the horse represented mobility, a source of income, and often, on the vast Western plains, a means of survival. Consequently, most of the collectibles associated with the range rider are also related to his horse. Spurs, bits, and bridles were the equipment a cowboy used to control his often cantankerous mount, while the saddle provided him with comfort and security through the long range days and a passable pillow at night.

The wrangler spent his hard-earned dollars to buy these handcrafted items. Custom-made, elaborately embossed saddles might cost a year's pay, far more than the average cayuse or range horse would bring; hence the old phrase "forty-dollar saddle on a ten-dollar horse." Metal bits and

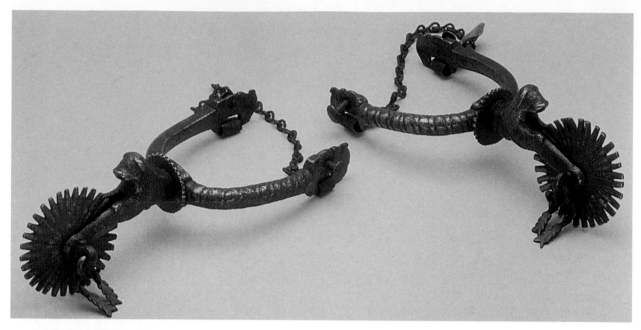

Many early cowboys used Spanish American spurs and bits, like this pair of early Southwestern wrought-iron spurs, c. 1750–1820, with a dog's-head motif. Spurs such as these were made both in northern Mexico and in the area that later became the southwestern United States. *Sherwoods Spirit of America: Butterfield and Butterfield*

spurs, despite their smaller size, provided a surface upon which the craftsman could work his art. Inlay, engraving, mixed metals, and unusual shapes were available—for a price.

From the collector's viewpoint, the decorative aspect of such gear is greatly enhanced by the fact that many makers marked their products, branding or stamping their names into both leather and metal. While enthusiasts for Native American crafts must generally deal with anonymous objects, the cowboy fan is often able to assemble a collection with a known origin.

SPURS

U-shaped spurs, with a long shank and a wheel-shaped rowel that often resembled a star, fit around the boot heel and were used to guide a horse. Though they might look menacing, the rowels were seldom sharp, and only in the most extreme circumstances would a cowboy dig them into his horse's

A pair of steel spurs of the "gal leg" type are inlaid in brass and were made by McChesney about 1900–1920. The presence of the original tooled leathers and packing box substantially increases the value of this set. *Sherwoods Spirit of America: Butterfield and Butterfield*

flanks. Nor were they usually worn when the cowboy was afoot. The Hollywood image of spur-clad buckaroos clanking up and down the wooden sidewalks of an imaginary Western town would seem ludicrous to an old hand.

But spurs were more than tools. They were status symbols. Many a westerner invested a substantial portion of his monthly pay in a finely wrought, decorated pair from a well-respected maker such as G.S. Garcia of Elko, Nevada, or A.B. Hunt of Caliente, California. Their marks meant quality and for today's enthusiast, they mean collectibility.

Spurs were made of a variety of materials such as wrought and cast iron, stainless steel, monel steel, nickel silver, brass, copper, and combinations of these—often with inlay in sterling silver and rowels cut from U.S. half-dollars. The basic form could be modified. Shanks might take the form of a woman's leg (the popular "gal leg type"), a bird's head, or a rattlesnake. Popular engraved or embossed images included horseheads, eagles, and the pips (diamonds,

These wrought-iron spurs with embossed and incised silver mountings in the form of hearts and conchos was made and marked about 1900–1910 by G. S. Garcia of Elko, Nevada. Spurs like these are top of the line with collectors of cowboy memorabilia. *Sherwoods Spirit of America: Butterfield and Butterfield*

This pair of roughly 1900 iron and leather spurs inlaid with chrome steel is tough and rust resistant. Steel was frequently used in the making of spurs.
Michael Friedman

hearts, clubs, spades) from a deck of playing cards.

Though they might look very similar to the novice collector, spurs were produced in a variety of distinct regional styles—California, Northern Plains, Texas, and the like—while shanks might be long or short, "gooseneck" or S-shaped. There are also many known makers including Main & Winchester of San Francisco, Kelly Brothers and Parker of Dalhart, Texas, J. O. Bass of Tulia, Texas, and the much-admired August Buermann. A maker's mark will always enhance the value of a set of spurs.

BITS

Bits, which are roughly H-shaped, are placed in a horse's mouth; the reins attached to them allow the rider to direct the horse. They were often manufactured by the same individuals who made spurs and were also elaborately decorated. One of the earliest makers, José de Jesus Mardueno of Carpenteria, California, who was active during the 1860s, turned out examples covered with floral engraving. His competitors—including Ralph Gutierrez of Cheyenne, Wyoming, L.D. Stone of San Francisco, and such firms as the Western Bit and Spur Company—produced even more elaborate forms.

Bits available to collectors may include ones whose shanks are in the form of the

A pair of iron, brass, and leather spurs decorated with hearts dates to the late nineteenth century. For the lonely cowpuncher, the heart design had a special poignancy.
Michael Friedman

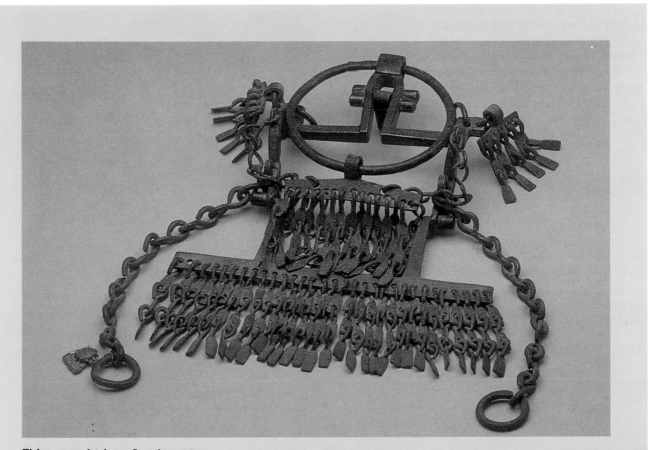

This wrought-iron Southwestern colonial ring bit, dates from 1770 to 1810. Elaborate bits such as this were used in the early days along the Rio Grande. They are seldom found today. *Sherwoods Spirit of America: Butterfield and Butterfield*

This unusual bit was made in the early twentieth century by Prisoner #9647 at the Colorado State Prison. It is made of wrought iron overlaid with engraved nickel and with abalone shell inlay. The six-guns may be the reason that #9647 ended up in prison! *Sherwoods Spirit of America: Butterfield and Butterfield*

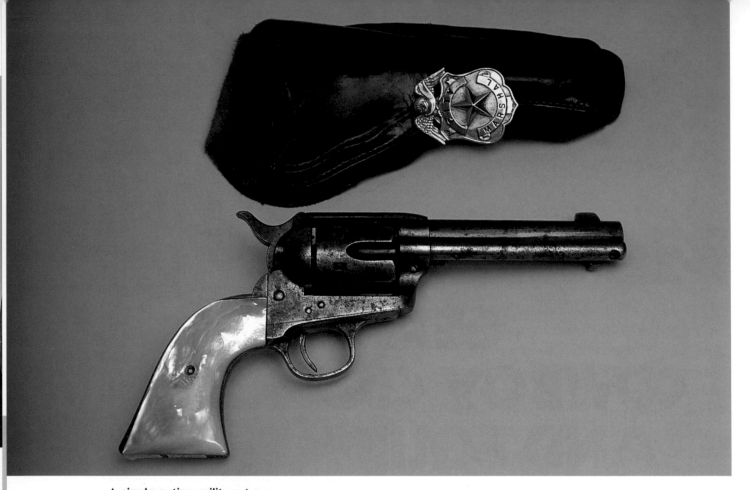

A single-action military-type .41-caliber six-gun with steel and mother-of-pearl grips is shown with its leather holster and a brass-and-pot metal marshal's star. All date to the late nineteenth century. *Michael Friedman*

WEAPONS

owboys and their guns are the stuff that the mythology of the West is made of. A wide variety of handguns and rifles was used there. Though most guns were never fired in anger, at least not at another human being, all are considered collectible. The legendary gunmen—Billy the Kid, Bat Masterson, Jesse James, et al.—were not ranch hands. Some may have worked the range, but it was usually to steal another man's cattle. Others were gamblers, lawmen, outlaws, or in some cases, all of the above at different times in their checkered careers. These were the people who perfected the fast draw, the accuracy, and the ruthlessness necessary to become killers.

The cowboy was not a killer. Indeed, because he lived at close quarters with others for long periods of time and cooperated in performing highly specialized tasks, having a reputation for sporting an itchy trigger finger would be a quick way to lose a trail job. That is not to say, though, that cowboys did not get into gunfights. Most were drinkers and some were gamblers. Others frequented the brothels of the cow towns. These were all activities that often led to violence, such as the 1871 shoot-out in a Newton, Kansas, bar that left nine men dead in less than five minutes. Most of the victims that night were cowboys, and in gunfights with gamblers or professional killers the brave but less experienced buckaroos usually came out on the short end.

However, the ranch hand did have a real need for weapons. Some of the cattle-driving trails such as the Chisholm and the Western passed through the lands of hostile Indian tribes, and rustlers were always a possibility. Even if these dangers were not present, firearms were useful for hunting game, killing rattlers or other dangerous animals, or just putting a sick or injured horse out of its misery.

For these purposes most cowboys used a rifle; many did not even carry handguns. One of the favorite long guns was the Winchester .44–.40-caliber, an 1873 model twelve- or fifteen-shot repeating rifle. Inexpensive, reliable, and accurate at a great distance, it has been referred to as "the gun that won the West." Other popular models were the .50-caliber Spencer rifle and the rolling block Remington .44-caliber. Both of these were originally military weapons, not an uncommon thing in an area where many of the first cowpunchers were Civil War veterans who had brought their equipment with them.

There was a much greater variety of handguns than rifles. Cowboys who could afford nothing better carried surplus army

The two handguns shown are the sort frequently carried by cowboys. At left is a model 1890 .44–.40-caliber Remington six-gun and at right, a double-action .40-caliber six-gun by Smith & Wesson. Unlike the majority of such weapons, these handguns are plated in silver and gold and have pearl handles. They are rare presentation pieces, not intended for use.
Private collection

Note the name CASE stamped on the wooden handle of this sheet steel 1900–1910 hunting knife. The Case company was one of the major knife manufacturers during the cowboy era, and nearly every cowhand carried a "Case." *Private collection*

Both the cowboy shirt and riding pants or jodhpurs date to about 1950–1970. While an outfit like this suits the rodeo circuit or the dude ranch, traditional cowboys were glad to settle for an old wool or flannel shirt and a pair of jeans. *Private collection*

weapons such as the Remington models .36- and .44-caliber percussion types. These were both heavy and slow: the ill-fated General George Custer was carrying a .44 Remington at the Little Big Horn. The manufacture in 1872 of Samuel Colt's famed six-shooter, a .45-caliber single-action revolver, marked a distinct advance in technology. Though it was often referred to as the "Peacemaker," this fast and accurate weapon brought little peace to the Western cow towns.

Among the other popular pistols were the .44-caliber Smith & Wesson American (the weapon carried by Buffalo Bill Cody), the .36-caliber percussion Colt (Wild Bill Hickok's favorite), the Hammond .44-caliber Bulldog, the .44-caliber Colt Dragoon, and the Colt New Army Model .38-caliber, first issued in 1896.

All these guns were used by ranch and trail hands, but it is usually not possible to associate them with any particular cowboy. It is important to keep in mind that during the last quarter of the nineteenth century, almost every male in the West owned a gun. As one Texan remarked, "I would as soon go out in the street without my pants as without my Colt."

Every cowhand also carried a knife, used not for self-defense but for eating, skinning game, cutting rope or brush, or just plain whittling. The large bowie knife,

COWBOY COLLECTIBLES

This pair of c. 1930–1940 leather women's cowboy boots made by the Kirkendall manufacturing company are typical of the boots worn by Eastern and Western dudes. *Private collection*

referred to by some as the "Arkansas toothpick," was not a cowboy knife. It was too large and awkward to have any practical value except in fighting. Most cowhands preferred a small knife with a five- to seven-inch blade. This was often locally made and would have a wooden or hard leather handle. Pocketknives such as the well-known Barlow knife were also an almost universal possession. As with guns, these blades were owned by almost all Western males. Still, examples identified with an individual cowpoke are hard to come by.

CLOTHING

Cowboys adopted a distinct mode of dress that was patterned on that of the Spanish-speaking *vaqueros* who had first ridden the wide Western plains. Their clothing was designed not for beauty but for practicality. Boots, hats, chaps, belts, and bandannas, the chief elements of such an outfit, all had a purpose. But they also created a distinct look, one which has become linked inseparably with the cowboy mystique through the medium

Ranch hands rather than dudes wore footwear like the pair of late-nineteenth-century stitched leather cowboy boots shown here. Few such early examples have survived. *Michael Friedman*

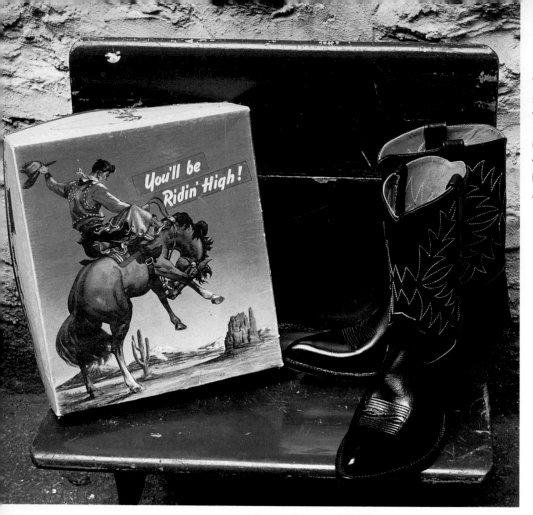

The leather cowboy boots shown here, of cowhide with fancy stitchwork, date to 1940–1950. The classic Western riding boot has changed little over the years. Pre-1920 examples, however, are hard to come by. *Private collection*

of film classics such as *High Noon* and *Stagecoach*, and which even impressed other early Westerners. A resident of Cheyenne, Wyoming, saw it thus in 1873:

> I observed . . . a drove of ridgy-spined long horn cattle which had been several months eating their way from Texas with their escort of four or five much-spurred horsemen in peaked hats, blue hooded coats and high boots, heavily armed with revolvers and repeating rifles.

Boots

The riding boot with narrow toe, thin sole, high heel, and decorative stitch work remains popular with modern-day riders, but few realize why it is constructed as it is. Boots were made high to protect the leg from rough brush and to prevent entry of sand and gravel. The sharp toe facilitated picking up the near stirrup on a rapidly turning horse. Stitching stiffened the soft leather so it would not curl over or wrinkle at the ankle, and the high heel kept a rider's foot from slipping through the stirrup.

Like saddles, bits, and spurs, boots became status symbols among cowhands. Many pairs were custom-made, often by the same firms that manufactured other Western leather goods. Stitchery, embossing, and engraving could be used to produce complex floral work or a complete scene. However, the most elaborate examples were not made for working hands, but for tourists and well-to-do Westerners impressed by the boots worn in movies of the 1920s and 1930s. These usually bring the highest prices as collectibles.

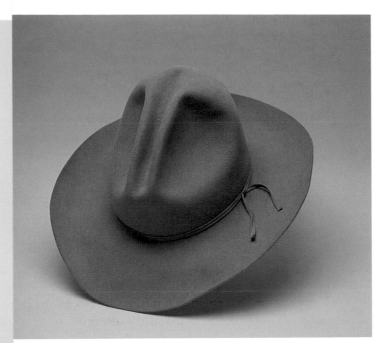

This early-1900s suede
Southwestern sombrero
is the classic cowboy hat.
Michael Friedman

Later boots such as these
cowhide cowboy boots for
women and children, c. 1940–
1960, have recently become
popular with collectors. Note
the elaborate stitchwork and
cutouts on these pairs.
Private collection

Hats

Cowboy hats, made from felt or other soft leather by firms such as Stetson, assumed their characteristic form in response to local conditions. The high crown provided insulation to keep the cowboy's head cool on the hot range; the wide brim (even wider in the Southwest) served as a sunshade and a sort of umbrella. The headgear, usually tan or gray, might also be put to use as a drinking vessel for a thirsty man or his horse, or as an easily seen signal.

Cowboys were fond of their hats and wore them down to nothing. As a result, pre-1900 examples are extremely hard to come by. Much more available are the 1930s type popularized by Tom Mix and other radio and cinema buckaroos. Like other late pseudo-cowboy gear, such items are often referred to by dealers and collectors as "cowboy funk."

As his actual role declined, the cowboy was seen as a symbol of romance and humor. This exaggerated carved and painted boot trade sign once graced the entrance to an early twentieth-century shoe store. *Private collection*

The term *cowboy kitsch* is attached to a variety of objects with a Western flavor that bear no actual connection to a cowhand's life. This 1930s cigarette box of plastic wood (sawdust mixed with glue) is a good example of well-crafted cowboy memorabilia. *Stephanie A. Ross*

A 1
whi
tass
typi
spir
the
in W
Priv

prisingly high prices. These latter items may include collectibles such as hats, chaps, boots, and other garb, saddles and horse tack, weapons, and even vehicles that can be associated with an important film or a well-known hero or even a notorious bad man of the silver screen.

It might also be mentioned that during an even earlier era cowboys, like Indians, served to promote patent medicines and cure-alls, which led to the production of bottles and advertising materials featuring some of the better-known (and some of the lesser-known) Western figures. Buffalo Bill Cody's popularity probably sold more than one bottle of Yosemite Yarrow or Wonder Worker, but it is doubtful, however, that the name of Texas Charley could do much for Sagwa; and, considering his own fate, Gen-

A mantel clock of bronzed spelter or white metal on a bakelite base from the 1940s has numerous Western motifs, including a horse, hat, boots, gun, and lariat. *Robert Weltz*

eral Custer's recommendation of Simmons' Liver Medicine probably fell on deaf ears!

OTHER COWBOY-RELATED OBJECTS

The number of products with a Western theme produced during the first half of this century is so extensive that it would be possible for a person to build an impressive collection just by focusing on a single area or a single material such as glass.

Toys alone offer a fertile collecting field. During the 1920–1950 era, nearly every actor who had played a role in a Western movie lent his or her name to children's playthings. There were Lone Ranger

Though hardly a Remington or a Russell, this bronzed cast-iron bookend is a good representation of the cowboy and his mount. On the reverse it is marked "1930 Cowboy and Broncho." *Author's collection*

masks, hats, and cowboy suits; Tom Mix six-guns (first made of metal, then of plastic); numerous representations of the famous horses Silver and Trigger; and Dale Evans cowgirl dolls. All are highly collectible today.

Household objects compose an even more extensive category. Particularly during the hard times of the 1930s, nostalgia for the Old West—or what was imagined to have been the Old West—ran deep. Representations of cowboys, horses, ranch houses, and similar Western themes were grafted onto clocks, parlor lamps, ashtrays, cigarette boxes, lighters, and dozens of other objects. Among the more interesting items were sets of cocktail glasses decorated with decals of cowgirls in scanty costumes. When a cold drink was poured into a glass, what little the women wore vanished.

In the clothing field, bucking broncos appeared on neckties and shirt fronts, suede vests took on a frontier fringe, and cuff links, tie clasps, and women's shoes and purses bore Western motifs. Fortunately, many of these items have survived and are available today at modest prices.

What should also be particularly appealing to the would-be collector is the fact that much of the 1920–1960 cowboy kitsch material can still be found at yard and tag sales or through visits to secondhand stores, church bazaars, and flea markets. Time, energy, and knowledge can be more important here than a fat wallet!

The cowboy has long been a popular twentieth-century doll form. This 1940–1950 cowboy doll is unusual in that it is entirely knitted. The body is stuffed with kapok, and the lariat is of twine.
The Strong Museum

This Shirley Temple cowgirl, made by Ideal Toy Company in 1936, has a composition body, mohair wig, leather vest, chaps, boots, cotton plaid shirt, and felt hat. Since Temple was one of the most popular movie stars of the 1930s, she was a natural to promote the cowgirl image.
The Strong Museum

hardship of life in the Southwest. Textiles from the Rio Grande area were next to gain recognition outside the immediate region; and with the rise of the so-called Santa Fe style, the crudely made but brightly colored furniture of New Mexico, Colorado, and Arizona began to appear in homes and apartments from Los Angeles to Bar Harbor.

Though decorating with Southwestern art, textiles, and furnishings often leads to jarring arrangements, when correctly done it provides us with the flavor of a culture that, like that of the Native Americans, is largely alien to most Americans.

The field, however, presents the collector with some problems. First, the amount of legitimate material is limited. The Spanish-speaking culture of the Southwest has never been large, and it has always been poor. The number of locally made religious paintings (*retablos*) and carvings (*bultos*) that have survived is small. Moreover, these can be confused with similar examples from Mexico, Puerto Rico, and South America.

One must buy with knowledge and from knowledgeable dealers.

Textiles too are in short supply and may resemble fabrics produced just across the Mexican border. Even harder to come by are authentic specimens of Spanish American furniture. The number of forms was always limited to chairs, tables, chests, bedsteads, and *trasteros,* or cupboards. Most were made from soft pine and have long since vanished. Nineteenth-century examples are uncommon, though a surprising number of pieces dating from about 1900 to 1930 in the harshly bright reds, yellows, and blues typical of the area are emerging from isolated homesteads.

There are also a limited number of artisans working in the old manner making bultos, chairs, and, particularly in the Chimayo region, fabrics. Moreover, some descendents of bulto makers, like Felipe Archuleta of Tesuque, New Mexico, have turned to the carving of secular folk figures, primarily animals.

FOLK ART OF THE SOUTHWEST

espite the present enthusiasm for American folk art, many people overlook the fact that the most coherent body of naive painting and sculpture produced in this country is the religious art of the Spanish Southwest. It is also among the oldest.

Spanish-speaking people from Mexico began to settle in New Mexico and surrounding areas in 1598, bringing with them their Catholic religion and the sacred paintings and statuary, which served both as supports for liturgical services and as symbols of the Divine Presence. As early as 1624 a list of materials supplied to Franciscan missionaries included such objects as altar sculpture and oil paintings to adorn church walls.

However, the tiny settlements in New Mexico were far from such major population centers as Mexico City, and much of the early religious art (which had been brought from Spain or created in the South . . . what was then known as "New Spain") was destroyed in the Pueblo Indian rebellion of 1680.

Once the area was retaken in 1692, the Spanish-speaking populace were largely thrown back upon their own resources and upon the creative skills of missionary priests and the occasional itinerant artist. These people were called upon to satisfy the need for religious paintings and sculpture, not only in the various missionary churches spreading across New Mexico but also in the numerous home shrines, or *nichos*, found in every community.

Artists primarily created three basic forms; large altar screens, panel paintings (retablos), and carvings (bultos). There were also seventeenth-century frescoes or wall paintings that in methods and materials (though not subject matter, which was

European) reflected the influence of Pueblo kiva painting and images on animal hide that appear to have been used by missionaries seeking to convert the natives. Practically all the early wall paintings have disappeared, and the few dozen remaining works on hide are in museum collections; so these offer few opportunities for the hopeful collector.

Most sought after today are the bultos and retablos, collectively termed santos. The former are carved and painted figures of saints based on medieval southern European forms but often reflecting Native American influence. Most bultos were carved in the round from local cottonwood root or slabs of ponderosa pine. The face (which was often given glass or ceramic eyes) was sometimes carved separately and then glued on, and the hands were tenoned into the wrists. The figure was next coated with gesso or artist's plaster and completed in one of two techniques.

With one known as *estofado,* details of dress and form were etched in the gesso,

SPANISH AMERICAN CRAFTS

These carved and painted cottonwood bultos of San Antonio and *(right)* Santa Rita are from Taos, New Mexico. Made between 1850 and 1865 by an unknown *santero,* they are typical of the religious art made for Spanish American churches and home shrines. *Taylor Museum, Colorado Springs Fine Arts Center*

This mid-nineteenth-century carved and painted cottonwood bulto is probably from San Antonio, New Mexico. The figure is missing both its hands, which were carved separately and then pinned to the body. *Museum of American Folk Art*

and the figure was then gilded and finished with water-based pigments. In the second, or *polychromado,* method, the artist bypassed etching and painted and gilded directly on the figure. This less sophisticated method was most frequently used in New Mexico.

While most bultos were fully developed figures, there were also the bultos *a vestir,* which were frameworks upon which simple wool or cotton clothing or vestments were hung. On these bultos the head, hands, and sometimes the feet were fully delineated; the body, concealed beneath its robe, was a stick figure. The full-form bultos were usually smaller, up to two feet in height, while the bultos *a vestir* were often as tall as four feet. The latter were frequently used in religious processions, particularly among the Penitentes, a lay religious sect that practiced self-flagellation and simulated crucifixion.

Retablos are small panel paintings of saints or other religious figures, customarily done on wood. After 1850, when sheet tin became available, they might also be found on this material. Wooden examples were hand cut and smoothed, coated with gesso, and after they had been painted, covered with wax or a rosinlike finish.

Though there are over a thousand Catholic saints, New Mexican artists and their clients showed preference for a relatively limited number. Among these, in addition to the Holy Family, are included El Niño de Atocha, San Jeronimo, San Antonio, Santo Domingo, San Francisco, San Jose, San Isidro, and San Juan. All appear frequently in both sculpture and painting.

Altar screens, or *reredos*, are large compositions of painted panels and sometimes bultos, combined in an oblong construction typically placed at the rear of the church altar above an altar table. In most cases, since the altar would be devoted to a particular saint, the altar screen would consist of various representations of this individual. Most existing altar screens remain in local

churches or have been constructed in museum settings.

From the mid-eighteenth until the late nineteenth century, painters and sculptors, known as *santeros*, created a substantial body of Spanish American religious art. But, because it was not the custom for artists to sign their work, relatively few existent pieces can be identified. There are, though, a handful of known *santeros* and these serve to also indicate some of the changes in style that took place even in such an isolated and traditional area as New Mexico.

With imported religious art difficult to obtain, some of the Franciscan friars who staffed the missions turned to painting and carving and to instructing native converts in these arts. One of the best known is Fray Andrés García, who was active from about 1748 to about 1778. Like many *santeros*, he made both bultos and retablos. The work of

This carved and painted cottonwood bulto of the Holy Family (c. 1979) is by Feliz Lopez, Espanola, New Mexico. Lopez is one of the most important figures in the late-twentieth-century revival of Spanish American sculpture. *Museum of American Folk Art*

SPANISH AMERICAN CRAFTS

Nearly life-size figures like this carved and painted cottonwood figure of the Nazarene Christ were carried in Holy Week processions. This figure, c. 1850–1860, with cotton robe and horsehair wig, is four feet high and is from northern New Mexico. *Taylor Museum, Colorado Springs Fine Arts Center*

A carved and painted cottonwood or pine figure of the Nazarene Christ has a horsehair wig and burlap sackcloth robe; it was made in northern New Mexico about 1850–1870. These large figures are usually associated with the Penitente Brotherhood. *Taylor Museum, Colorado Springs Fine Arts Center*

Altar screens were part of the furnishings of Southwestern churches, but because of their size and fragility, few have survived. This example, of carved and painted wood (c. 1840–1890), is a reconstruction of the one in the chapel of Our Lady of Talpa, Talpa, New Mexico.
Taylor Museum, Colorado Springs Fine Arts Center

García and his fellows is sometimes referred to as "provincial academic," reflecting the fact that they relied heavily upon copying traditional Spanish styles.

The first artist to move toward an indigenous style was the so-called Laguna *santero* (a name taken from his best-documented work, the altar screen at the church in Laguna Pueblo). Working in the late eighteenth and early nineteenth century, he abandoned perspective and realism for a two-dimensional treatment of his subject matter. He also established a workshop or *taller* based on the European plan, in which artworks were made cooperatively by a variety of masters, journeymen, and apprentices. Many later *santeros* followed this tradition, making it often difficult to determine if a piece is by a major *santero* or by one of his followers.

Other early nineteenth-century New Mexican artists who may have been followers of or influenced by the Laguna master include "Molleno" (working 1815–1845), whose paintings and altar screens show a severe and impersonalized spiritual imagery seemingly related to American Indian painting. Indeed, there is some evidence that this man, about whom little other than a name is known, may have been a native or of mixed ancestry.

Also thought to be of Indian origin is the so-called Quill Pen Santero (c. 1830–1850), who is believed to have worked in Molleno's *taller* but who developed his own distinct retablo style characterized by strong calligraphic outlines and bright colors.

The most famous artist of the mid-nineteenth century was José Aragón (c. 1820–1835), a man who had the foresight to sign many of his paintings, thus making himself an object of attention for both scholars and collectors. Much more academic than many of his fellows, Aragon produced retablos in a simple, naturalistic style, many of which were based on period Mexican engravings.

Another "provincial academic" artist, José Rafael Aragón (c. 1820–1862) was probably the most popular santero of his period. Usually called Rafael Aragón (no known relation to José Aragón), he worked

This retablo of the Mater Dolores, tempera on cottonwood, was painted between 1830 and 1850 by José Rafael Aragón of New Mexico. Aragón is considered to be one of the finest artists among the retablo painters. *Taylor Museum, Colorado Springs Fine Arts Center*

This retablo of San Juan Nomucene, of tempera on a cottonwood panel, was made about 1820–1830 in northern New Mexico. It is attributed to the "AJ" santero since these initials appear on several related retablos. *Taylor Museum, Colorado Springs Fine Arts Center*

Attributed to the Santo Niño Santero is this tempera-on-cottonwood retablo of the Mater Dolores made in Chimayo, New Mexico, about 1830–1840. Nearly all early Southwestern retablos are on wood, though examples on tin and glass are common in Mexico and Central America. *Taylor Museum, Colorado Springs Fine Arts Center*

both in Santa Fe and in what is now Cordova, New Mexico, producing an array of altar screens, bultos, and retablos. His bold lines and bright colors had great appeal for both church and lay customers, and some authorities see him as the best of the New Mexican santeros.

A popular folk artist, Aragón had many disciples, including one known only as the Santo Niño Santero, whose simple, abstract work includes delicate carvings generally regarded as the most technically sophisticated of New Mexican bultos.

The production of santos gradually went into decline after 1850 as Anglo-Saxons moved into New Mexico, bringing with them new attitudes and new art images of inexpensive and brightly colored religious lithographs, which could be purchased for a penny or two apiece. However, in the 1920s, museum and collector interest led to a revival of the craft. Santeros such as Felíz Lopez, José Dolores Lopez, Horacio Valdéz, and Leo Salazar have produced carvings that maintain the ancient traditions even though most of their output is sold to Anglo collectors rather than to Spanish Americans.

SPANISH AMERICAN CRAFTS

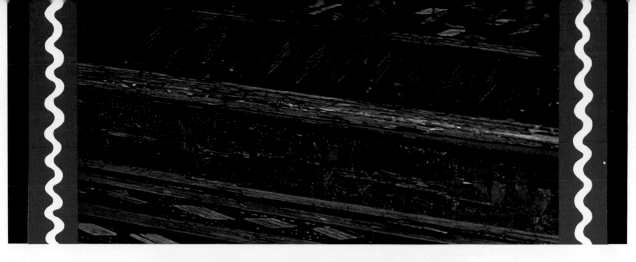

FURNITURE, FURNISHINGS, AND TEXTILES

ompared to settlers in other areas of this country, the Spanish American pioneers of the Southwestern states always had relatively few belongings. As a consequence, collectible items are limited primarily to santos, a few simple household furnishings, and some remarkable but hard-to-come-by woven textiles.

What does remain seems frozen in time. Things made in the nineteenth or even early twentieth century are in a much earlier style, often appearing medieval in form. There is good reason for this. The settlers who in the late sixteenth and early seventeenth centuries pushed into the deserts and hills of Texas, Arizona, and New Mexico were Iberians of a most conservative bent. They brought with them furniture styles, weaving

Seating furniture like this piñon pine stool, New Mexico, c. 1870–1900, was usually put together without nails or screws, which local craftsmen regarded as too expensive. *Private collection*

methods, and habits of work that had been handed down at home for generation after generation.

This alone is not unusual. A similar situation prevailed in Mexico City or in Boston or New York at the same time. The difference, however, is that as technology and taste changed in Europe, innovations flowed directly to these major cities. What sociologists call "cultural lag" became shorter and shorter until by the early 1800s, a new Paris or Barcelona gown, hairdo, or furniture style would reach New Orleans or Caracas in a few weeks. This was not true in Santa Fe, which was so far removed from the seat of Spanish rule that it was almost forgotten. Indeed, after the Mexican republic was declared in 1821, the citizens were left largely to take care of themselves.

FURNITURE

Thrown back on their own resources and faced with both an often hostile climate and limited building materials, local craftsmen produced but a few furniture forms: stools, chairs, tables, chests, and the distinctive galleried cupboards known as trasteros. Almost all were formed from locally available softwoods, principally piñon pine and cottonwood. Since both woods were soft and relatively fragile, furnishings had to be massive and the carving extremely broad and shallow. Because sixteenth-century Iberian furnishings had been made from timber of remarkably similar characteristics, local craftsmen were at home with both the medium and the style.

Cut off from outside influences, *carpinteros* continued to produce seventeenth-century furniture types until the late nineteenth or early twentieth century, when

A detail of the wrought-iron lock and latch on this chest shows that llke their Spanish ancestors, Southwestern craftsmen were highly skilled ironworkers. *Taylor Museum, Colorado Springs Fine Arts Center*

Old red paint is still evident on this piñon pine storage chest from New Mexico, c. 1860–1880. This piece was constructed with dovetailed corners and is pegged on the bottom. Chests like this took the place of closets and chests of drawers in the Southwestern home. *Taylor Museum, Colorado Springs Fine Arts Center*

A straw-work storage box from Santa Fe, New Mexico, dates to 1880–1910. The technique of inlay in straw was brought from Europe by early settlers and has been practiced in Santa Fe for generations. *Taylor Museum, Colorado Springs Fine Arts Center*

This small tripod table with a pine top, and a base of carved cottonwood root all covered in an old red stain, was made in New Mexico about 1880–1910. Rural craftsmen often used natural forms like this in furniture construction. *Private collection*

all but a few isolated chair makers were driven out of business by the cheap and beguilingly "modern" factory furniture being brought in by railroad from the East.

Because both methods and materials remained the same over a long period (wood was hand cut and planed until after 1850 and cost largely prohibited the use of iron nails, screws, or hinges), it is frequently difficult to determine the age of a piece of Southwestern furniture. Much that is sold as "early 1800s" was actually made fifty to a hundred years later. Hand-plane marks, leather or wooden hinges, and pegged construction are good clues to earlier examples.

FURNISHINGS

The Southwestern home was small, and cooking utensils, storage boxes, lighting devices, and the like never existed in any great quantity. However, locally made furnishings reflected Iberian traditions. Boxes, made of roughly joined boards, might serve to store a few bits of precious jewelry or, in

An unpainted chopping bowl of oak or pine, New Mexico, dates from the middle to late nineteenth century. Large bowls like this were used to prepare and serve meals. They were often made at home from the trunks of trees. *Private collection*

a much larger form, clothing, wheat, or animal fodder. Early examples, left unfinished, were carved with shallow relief designs of lions or flowers or simple geometric devices. By the 1800s paint was commonly used, usually in broad areas of red or blue; less often there were conventionalized floral or geometric designs copied from Mexican or imported Chinese furnishings.

Cooking and serving utensils, bowls, plates, and platters were also carved from local woods as were such basic necessities as the mortar and pestle, the churn, and even the small closed vessels that held the hunter's powder and shot.

Two distinctive nineteenth-century Spanish craft traditions, found nowhere else in the United States, were straw and leather work. Using the former, the craftsman would cover the surface of a small box, picture frame, religious cross, or book stand with a thick paste of rosin and soot, which dried to a shiny black surface simulating lacquer. Into the wet paste he would press split stems of straw or corn husk, which, once the paste had dried, were cut

Incised geometric designs decorate a carved cottonwood powder or shot flask from New Mexico, made about 1850–1880. Spanish Americans also made powder or shot pouches from leather. *Private collection*

Though possibly a toy, this donkey is more likely a crèche figure. Of carved and painted cottonwood, it was made in New Mexico about 1860–1890. *Private collection*

into geometric and floral patterns that completely covered the piece. The golden straw, glittering in the feeble light of a candle or fat lamp, was often termed "poor man's gilding."

Rawhide leather, imported from Mexico or obtained from bison and longhorn cattle, was cut into long strips, then woven into everything from traveling trunks and storage boxes to hammocks, saddle trappings, and even window curtains. Few such items can be found today.

Metalwork has long been an Iberian tradition. Iron was always rare in the Southwest, but what could be obtained was frequently converted into small lamps to burn animal fat or into strong locks and latches for doors and chests. Once the Santa Fe Trail was opened in the 1850s, Anglos brought tin, usually in the form of tin cans,

This Rio Grande–style blanket of woven wool from New Mexico dates about 1940–1960. Though they have largely been overshadowed by Native American weavings in the past, New Mexican textiles are now beginning to attract wide collector attention.
Private collection

which was recycled into everything from picture frames to candlesticks, lanterns, and panels upon which retablos were painted. Such work is often difficult to distinguish from Mexican forms, though the latter tend to be more elaborately decorated and to feature glass fragment inlay.

TEXTILES

Sixteenth-century settlers introduced sheep into the Southwest, and were the first to weave woolen textiles. Their small horizontal harness looms could produce only narrow strips of cloth, little more than two feet wide. Since these were typically stitched together to produce the standard textile forms, blankets and shawls, mattress ticking, and floor cover-

ings, they can be distinguished from both Navajo and Mexican textiles, which were much wider and lack the sewn seam.

The best-known Southwestern textiles are the so-called Rio Grande–style blankets —which feature complex geometric patterns in several colors and, unlike their Navajo counterparts, may have tufted fringes —and the embroidered blanket, or *colcha*. The latter, unique to the Spanish American culture, consists of a woven wool or cotton ground upon which abstract floral or geometric patterns are embroidered, also in wool. The finest colchas were used as bed covers, and nineteenth-century examples are highly prized.

The introduction during the late nineteenth century of factory-made textiles gradually destroyed the Southwestern weaving industry except in the Chimayo Valley near Santa Fe, New Mexico, where traditional craftspeople have adapted their work to satisfy the desires of collectors and tourists.

Shown is a front view of a beautiful woven wool jacket made in the Chimayo Valley near Santa Fe, New Mexico, about 1940–1960. Note the silk label at the neck. Unlike earlier Spanish American textiles, modern Chimayo products bear makers' marks. *Nina Ryan*

The back view of the jacket reveals complex geometric devices that are variations of traditional Rio Grande blanket patterns. *Nina Ryan*

MINING

NORTH BUTTE MINING COMPANY

SHARES $15 EACH.

NUMBER 15087

SHARES 10

INCORPORATED UNDER THE LAWS OF THE STATE OF MINNESOTA.

MEMORABILIA

The collecting of objects associated with the mines of the American West is relatively recent and is confined to a limited number of enthusiasts. One reason for this small market is that the objects involved, primarily tools and machinery, are not particularly attractive. Native American crafts have achieved a worldwide artistic reputation. Spanish American santos and textiles are also highly regarded, and the bits, spurs, and saddles used by cowboys were frequently embellished with great technical skill.

On the other hand, the Western miners who worked surface ore sites employed ordinary shovels, picks, pry bars, and pans that looked much like those used in other groundbreaking tasks, and the machinery, ore carts, pneumatic drills, rock crushers and the like used in gold and silver mills are both massive and unattractive to collectors other than the most devoted.

As a consequence, the collecting fraternity for mining memorabilia remains small and localized, concentrated in the areas in which the ore was mined. Certain items, however, appear to have a broader collector base. Stock certificates, which are both colorful and historic, have a wide appeal. Also, the few memorial pieces that were made, such things as miniature silver picks and shovels presented to mine owners or to retiring workers, are regarded as universally desirable.

Since there is no important national market for mining memorabilia, collectors usually seek out the objects in states such as California, Colorado, or Nevada, where they would have been used. Some items are recovered from abandoned mine sites—not a recommended method of collecting since these are both privately owned and often dangerous. Others may be purchased from secondhand stores or the families of those who took part in the Gold Rush. As a general rule, prices remain quite reasonable as compared to those in other fields of Western Americana.

MINERS' EQUIPMENT

HAND TOOLS AND CLOTHING

The "forty-niners" and other early Western miners sought gold, which, because of its chemical composition, is often particularly susceptible to surface mining. Flakes or even small nuggets of the metal wash out of eroding bedrock and may be found in sandy streambeds. A prospector armed with nothing more than a shallow tin pan, in which sand and water can be swirled about until the heavier ore particles settle to the bottom, might find several hundred dollars' worth of this placer gold in a day.

Tales of gold panning have made the round tin vessels with sloping sides as synonymous with the miner as the six-gun is with the cowboy. Yet most such pans can hardly be distinguished from the nineteenth-century

A miner's gold pan, c. 1880–1910, is made of sheet tin. The term "panning" for gold reflected a procedure whereby gold-bearing sand was swirled in a miner's pan until the heavier particles of gold or "color" settled out. It was usually slow work! *Private collection*

Embossed on one side of this 1870–1890 blown-glass whiskey flask is FOR PIKE'S PEAK and the figure of a walking prospector. The other side pictures a hunter shooting a deer. Such pieces both memorialized and ridiculed the "forty-niners."
Author's collection

milk pans from which they were adapted. Fortunate indeed is the collector who can boast of a pan marked with a manufacturer's name or one with a reliable history of use in the gold fields.

Much the same may be said for the miner's other basic tools: the shovel, pickax, pry or crow bar, and sledgehammer. Any shovel available served to scoop up gold-bearing sand or dirt. Gold still lodged in cracks in the rock could be wrenched out with the crowbar or dislodged with a pickax, while ore found, as was often the case, in combination with quartz crystals could be broken free by blows from a sledgehammer.

These tools formed the equipment first of the miner who worked the "dry diggings"—rock outcrops and streamside cliffs —and later the hard-rock miner, who penetrated the earth's surface seeking wealth.

Much of the collectible mining material is associated with miners who toiled in the deep mines. They, or rather the corpora-

Early miner's lamps, from 1850 to 1870 include *left,* a candle lamp made of sheet iron and glass and, *right,* a covered candle lantern with brass case and glass "bull's-eye." The first hard-rock miners used whatever lighting devices were available. *Private collection*

tions that employed them, sought not only gold but also silver (found in combination as silver sulfide) and copper. All three minerals often had to be extracted from solid rock, which was itself removed from the earth at great depths.

The hard-rock miner's tools were, besides the earlier hand tools, the drill and dynamite. Initially, hand drills were employed to bore holes in which explosive charges were placed to shatter ore-bearing rock. By the 1880s, however, powerful pneumatic drills had been introduced. These are far more readily identified as mining-related than previous tools and are sought by serious collectors despite their substantial size and weight. The boxes and barrels in which sticks of dynamite and dynamite caps were stored and transported are also collectible, especially if they bear a stenciled manufacturer's logo.

With the exception of hard hats, introduced late in the nineteenth century, miner's clothing differed little from that worn by other manual laborers. The helmets, however, are distinctive and highly collectible. Early examples were of sheet steel or aluminum, but these were soon replaced by lighter ones made first from composition fiber and later from plastic, in both cases reinforced with steel. The mining helmet can usually be distinguished from similar headgear worn by construction workers by the hooks upon which a small light may be hung. Most sought after are those helmets that bear the names of Western mining companies.

LIGHTING DEVICES

Working far underground, the hard-rock miners required a variety of lighting devices. The earliest were candle holders and lanterns of the sort long used by iron, tin, and coal miners. These included the square candle lantern made of glass panels framed

A kerosene hand lamp like this one of sheet brass, dating from about 1880–1920, could either be held or attached to a nail driven into shaft wall. Kerosene was usually used to light tunnels that led to the working area. *Private collection*

This carbide safety lamp of sheet iron, brass, and glass dates from 1880 to 1930. Safety lamps that reduced the danger of explosion in the deep mines were gradually adopted throughout the West. They are among the more attractive and interesting of mining collectibles. *Private collection*

in wood and the "sticking Tommy," or pricket light. The latter, long associated with mining, consisted of a piece of wrought iron tapered to a point at one end and with the other formed to a cup, which would hold a candle. The sharpened spike could be wedged into a crack in the mine wall or pushed into a supporting wooden girder. Though they date back hundreds of years and provided little light, sticking Tommies were still being made as late as 1903, when a St. Louis, Missouri, hardware store offered them at $1 apiece.

Somewhat more efficient was the "fat lamp." Made of tin, it looked a bit like a small cylindrical coffeepot with a large spout in which a wick was laid as well as a hook by which it might be attached to a miner's helmet. Though smoky and foul smelling, fat lamps were for many years the best illumination available to the miner at the rock face.

The carbide lamp, which was intro-

A cast-iron mortar and pestle dates to about 1870–1900. These tools were used to grind ore samples in the assay office in order to determine if they were rich enough to justify exploitation of the claim. *Nina Ryan*

This small, c. 1900–1930 carbide lamp has a clip in the back in order that it may be attached to the hardhat worn by the miner. *Private collection*

duced in the late nineteenth century, proved to be a great improvement. These cylindrical brass lamps often had circular reflectors and cast a bright light. Most were made in England, but they are considered American mining collectibles and are much sought after.

Kerosene lamps of various sorts were also used in the mines from the 1870s on, though primarily to light tunnels and shafts rather than in work areas. Some examples, made of glass and sheet iron, are quite large. Nearly all were produced in this country.

After 1900, electric generators gradually replaced kerosene for lighting the tunnels, and the individual miner turned to battery-powered headlights, of which some of the earlier examples are considered collectible. As with other mining materials, lighting devices bearing company logos or some other evidence of their use below ground are always at a premium value.

This small portable scale from about 1860–1920 is of brass and steel. Scales like these were widely used in the days when debts were often paid in gold dust or nuggets.
Private collection

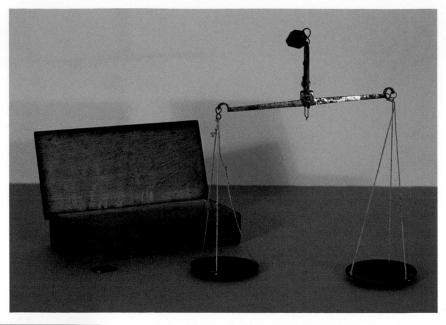

Small sets of iron and brass scales like these were used by grocers and warehouse and dry goods firms to weigh the gold dust and nuggets with which they often paid for food and supplies. This set dates to the late nineteenth century.
Private collection

ASSAYING EQUIPMENT

The tools and devices needed to determine the gold or silver content of ore and to weigh purified gold or silver bullion form an interesting area of collecting. Most popular with collectors are bullion scales. These come in many different forms, from the small iron or brass pocket scales used by miners in the field to elaborate assayer's or bank scales which might be housed in a glass and mahogany box. Many of the larger examples bear the mark of an American or English manufacturer.

Closely related are the the bags in which gold dust, bullion, or ore might be transported and the safes in which they were stored. An authentic example of a safe from a Wells Fargo office may bring several thousand dollars at auction.

There are also molds and tools such as mortars and pestles used by the professional assayers who determined if the ore content of a rock sample was sufficient to justify exploitation of a mining claim.

These assay office cased scales
of brass and iron, mounted
within a mahogany and glass
case, date to about 1870–1910.
Where finer work was required
at the bank, assay, or land claim
office, these delicately
balanced scales were used.
Private collection

Whitford, Andrew Hunter. *North American Indian Arts*. New York: Golden Press, 1970.

———. *Southwestern Indian Baskets: Their History and Their Makers*. Santa Fe, N.M.: School of American Research Press, 1988.

Wilder, Mitchell A., and Edgar Breitenbach. *Santos—The Religious Folk Art of New Mexico*. Colorado Springs: privately published, 1943.

Wilson, Maria Vergara. "New Mexican Textiles." *The Clarion* 13:4 (Fall 1988).

Wyatt, Victoria. *Shapes of Their Thoughts: Reflections of Cultural Contact in Northwest Coast Indian Art*. Norman: University of Oklahoma Press, 1984.

ACKNOWLEDGMENTS

The author gratefully acknowledges the assistance of the following individuals and institutions who contributed photographs and information for use in this book:

Museum of American Folk Art

Brooklyn Childrens' Museum

Frank Carbone

Virginia Chapman

University of Colorado Museum

Commission Mart

Mary K. Dahl

William Dobey

Michael Friedman

Anne Geisman

Pat Goldstein

Historic Mining and Milling Museum

Carl Hotkowiski

Sharon W. Joel

Michael D. Kokin/Sherwood's Spirit of America/Butterfield & Butterfield

Pendleton Wollen Mills, Inc.

Nina Ryan

Stephanie A. Ross

Helen and Ezra Stoller

The Strong Museum

Taylor Museum, Colorado Springs Fine Arts Center

Robert Weltz

Grateful thanks also go to Anne Edelstein, and to the people at Crown Publishers: my editor, Sharon Squibb, Betty Prashker, Michelle Sidrane, María Bottino, Joan Denman, and June Bennett-Tantillo. I would also like to thank Ann Cahn.